Teaching Children English as an Additional Language

A programme for 7–11 year olds

Caroline Scott

Routledge
Taylor & Francis Group

LONDON AND NEW YORK

First published 2009
by Routledge
2 Park Square, Milton Park, Abingdon, Oxon OX14 4RN

Simultaneously published in the US and Canada
by Routledge
270 Madison Avenue, New York, NY 10016

Routledge is an imprint of the Taylor & Francis Group, an informa business

Typeset in Mixage and AvanteGarde by
Keystroke, 28 High Street, Tettenhall, Wolverhampton

Printed and bound in Great Britain by
MPG Books Ltd, Bodmin, Cornwall

British Library Cataloguing in Publication Data
A catalogue record for this book is available from the British Library

Library of Congress Cataloging in Publication Data
Scott, Caroline, 1976–
Teaching children English as an additional language: a programme for
7–12 year olds/Caroline Scott.
     p. cm.
1. English language–Study and teaching–Foreign speakers.
2. Second language acquisition. I. Title.
PE1128.A2S324 2008
428.2'24–dc22   2007048580

ISBN 10: 0–415–45231–7 (pbk)
ISBN 10: 0–203–92656–0 (ebk)

ISBN 13: 978–0–415–45231–1 (pbk)
ISBN 13: 978–0–203–92656–7 (ebk)

Contents

Acknowledgements

I would like to thank Miss Sara Hassan for her efficiency, hard work and beautiful illustrations. Also a huge thank you to Dahlia Ferrer for her graphics advice and long hours spent organising and referencing all the illustrations. I am most grateful.

Thank you to the London Borough of Tower Hamlets for the Innovations Funding which allowed me to get this programme started. This support has given me the momentum to continue to develop it over the past five years.

Thanks to Helena Matthews, my mum, who has helped me with more aspects of this book than she realises. I am forever grateful for her ongoing professional and personal support. I cannot thank her enough for what she has done for me.

Thanks also to Karen Murray, John Matthews and Noha Bashir for helping me edit drafts of the programme.

Thank you also to Iain Scott, Sue Scott, Edd Scott, James Scott, Helena Matthews, John Matthews, Steve Matthews, Nick Matthews, Trish Donovan, Tom George, Adam Sefton and Lindsay Hunter for inspiring me to develop the characters in the programme.

Thanks to Lindsay Hunter and Tom George for helping me with the legalities.

Special thanks to Ahmed Rostom who has helped me overcome so many barriers in Egypt and to Shahira Yehia and Shady Remon who has made me feel so welcome in this country.

Thank you to Annette Rook, my former headteacher, who allowed me the freedom to develop my interests and inspired me to follow this path.

Thank you to the cover photographer, Michaela Adams, and the children who posed for the photographs at Cairo English School.

I am also grateful to the Qualifications and Curriculum Authority for permission to reproduce an extract from the QCA website – http://www.qca.org.uk/qca_5093.aspx and the 'Extended scale for EAL'.

Thanks also to Katherine Diaper, Jane Connolly, Peter Nathan, Zoe Smith, Pam Kaur, Leonie Hayes, Dawn Sedgewick, Julie Kimber and Su Weekes who have all played a part in the development of this book among many others. I have been very lucky to have such supportive people around me.

An introduction to teaching children English as an additional language (EAL)

Here's a scenario.

There are 30 children in a class. A third have spoken English all their lives and speak English at home. Two-thirds speak a different language at home and only speak English at school. Most of the latter pupils have a limited vocabulary and poor grammatically structured sentences. Five of these pupils have recently arrived in the country, they hardly understand anything the teacher says, they can't spell their names, and as a result of the language barrier and huge change in life circumstances, they are very easily distracted from tasks. Through differentiation, the class teacher has the very difficult job of providing the national curriculum for every child in this class.

This is a very real situation. I have been there and I managed to make it work. However, I did not have the time to consistently provide these EAL learners with the most effective teaching and learning experiences. I read copious amounts of information on how to accommodate these learners. Most gave good advice (QCA, 2004b) but they didn't provide easy solutions to support the new arrivals. In my opinion, this area has the potential for a curriculum of its own.

I have therefore written this programme for anyone who needs to support new arrivals and would like an 'easy to use' introduction to English for 7–11-year-old children. This could include class teachers, support staff, EAL staff or schools with limited provision for new arrivals. I hope you find it helpful.

EAL barriers to learning

So what are the issues?

Learners of English as an additional language need support in:

- Producing and understanding the sounds of English that differ from their first language
- Distinguishing between different sounds in English (e.g. bed/pet, hard/heart/art)
- Understanding oral sets of instructions
- Processing language that is expressed quickly
- Understanding and using appropriate intonation and stress
- Following whole group interactions
- Understanding and using statements, questions, offers and commands
- Understanding the meaning of particular language features in texts which we might take for granted, such as prepositions

(e.g. between, under) or adverbs (e.g. quite, very)

- Understanding oral texts not supported by visual/concrete cues
- Learning appropriate non-verbal communication
- Identifying the key words in a message
- Putting words in the right order
- Understanding new vocabulary, especially increasing technical language
- Understanding lexical metaphor (e.g. 'I'm pulling your leg', 'time flies')
- Learning the appropriate language for playing collaboratively
- Learning the appropriate language to interact socially with adults and peers
- Developing an understanding of appropriate school behaviour.

(DETE, nd)

With so many barriers to learning, it's hard to know where to start. The Qualifications and Curriculum Authority (QCA, 2004b) highlights three principles for developing an inclusive curriculum that can support teachers' planning for new arrivals. These are:

- Setting suitable learning challenges
- Responding to pupils' diverse learning needs

- Overcoming potential barriers to learning and assessment for individuals and groups of pupils.

In addition, they outline ways in which teachers can achieve successful planning as well as some useful strategies that can be used to teach new arrivals (see Chapter 4).

I have seen throughout my career many useful lists. However, I have yet to find a practical and effective way to address all the new arrivals' needs whilst committing myself to a time-consuming full-time teaching job. Time is of the essence and, with all due respect to every hard working teacher, I wonder how they find the time to plan effectively for the EAL learner.

This is a practical, easy to follow programme, complete with resources, for teachers with tight time constraints to help children learn English as an additional language. This book offers practical answers to help new students move into English quickly.

If you would like training in this programme please contact the author at postforcaroline@hotmail.com.

An introduction to the programme

How it works – in theory

This programme can be taught by an English as an additional language (EAL) teacher, class teacher or teaching assistant. It requires a 1 hour and 15 minutes withdrawal lesson every day (possibly during Literacy), which could be split into a 1-hour lesson and a 15-minute revision session at a different time in the day.

The programme is effective for EAL 'individuals or groups of pupils for finely tuned, time-limited withdrawal' (DfES, 2006a). It is finely tuned as it provides for the needs of individuals and groups of children, following a baseline assessment and an assessment for learning (see Appendices 2 and 4). It offers opportunities for learning through speaking and listening, practising, applying, extending and evaluating. Its duration is based on a pupil's understanding of key basic vocabulary and grammar structures and should be no more than 11 weeks.

This withdrawal programme offers good provision for EAL pupils. Such provision often cannot be made when one class teacher is expected to differentiate daily for such a huge range of learners. This is especially significant during a subject such as Literacy when one 11 year old may be reading a complex novel and another 11 year old is an EAL learner who may barely be able to read their own name. It isn't impossible, but who has the time?

Of course, it is important to emphasise that 'children learning EAL need to learn more than just vocabulary, grammar and pronunciation'. However, we can't ignore the children's distinct requirements for the basics in English. They are essential for fulfilling the learner's basic needs. 'Many bilingual children suffer low self-esteem because of early frustrations and language related difficulties in school. A cycle of failure, low self-esteem and subsequent expectations of continued failure must not be allowed to develop' (Gibbons, 1991). Children need to feel safe, settled, valued and have a sense of belonging to the class (DfES, 2002). The whole experience for a new arrival can be extremely stressful and we must do everything we can to support a smooth integration into their new English-speaking environment.

It's true to say that 'a major weakness of any pre-designed language course is that it remains a matter of chance whether or not the topic and structures of the course have anything to do with the actual language skills that learners need in their regular classes' (Gibbons, 1991). However, this programme has been developed to address this issue. It is flexible as the teacher can use it to identify the children's needs and encompasses continual assessment for learning.

In the case of very limited to zero exposure to the language, pre-course 'emergency language sessions' have been written into the programme to introduce new, useful language to children. This language wouldn't previously have been introduced at such an early stage; for example, past simple.

As the children make progress, they are able to use the basics in English and gradually extend the complexities of their understanding. They also need to 'learn to use their whole language repertoire appropriately for a range of different purposes' (DfES, 2006a). However, this takes time.

According to *Inspecting Subjects 3–11: English as an Additional Language* (Ofsted, 2000, quoted in QCA, 2004b):

> It takes on average five to seven years to become fully competent in a second language, although individuals will vary in the speed with which they acquire this competence. Fluency in spoken English is usually achieved within two years but the ability to read and understand more complex texts containing unfamiliar cultural references and to write the academic language needed for success in examinations takes much longer.

It is important to remember that this process will take time and children learning English as an additional language are going to need long-term support.

The programme is built on the principles of teaching and learning outlined by the DfES (2004):

- It sets high expectations and gives every learner confidence that they can succeed.
- It establishes what learners already know and builds on this.
- It is structured and paces the learning experience to make it challenging and enjoyable.
- It is designed to inspire children to learn.

- It makes individuals active participants in their learning.
- It develops learning skills and personal qualities.

The lessons should have a cycle of review, teach, practise, apply and evaluate (DfES, 2006b).

Research on children learning English as a second language (DfES, 2005) discusses different approaches to language learning. The findings showed there is no single, effective method of teaching a language. However, there is,

> Broad agreement about an approach to language teaching and learning which stresses the importance of communication in the language – real language use – as a central component of learning as well as a desired outcome for that learning . . . a rich and varied input of the new language together with opportunities for learners to interact with the language.

The research also outlined that speaking and listening allows children to 'organise and rehearse ideas in advance of putting them on paper' and it is a key factor in securing successful learning. There is a wealth of such advice on communication. For these reasons, learning through speaking and listening is incorporated into every lesson.

The use of the children's home language is another extremely important element of learning a language. Gibbons (1991) highlighted three reasons that have special significance:

1 It allows children to draw on their total language experience and so continue their conceptual development, making it easier for children to understand, and therefore

learn, the English related to these concepts.

2   It helps to provide a social-economic environment in which the basic conditions for learning can occur, and, therefore, also helps to lessen the trauma and alienation that children may experience in a new environment surrounded by an unknown language.

3   It is sound educational practice to build on a learner's competencies and abilities.

Special attention is given to learning in both languages within the programme and emphasis has been placed on acknowledging the translation either verbally or in writing, where possible, during every lesson.

Learning styles need special consideration. A learning style is a different approach or way of learning (Gardner, 1999):

- Visual – learning through seeing
- Auditory – learning through hearing
- Kinaesthetic – learning through doing, moving and touching.

Accommodations for learning styles are made through various mediums including gestures, picture resources and dialogue.

The benefits of the programme

The major benefits of the programme are:

- Teaching of fundamental grammar and vocabulary needed to speak English
- Assessment for learning
- Teaching new language through speaking and listening
- Provision of activities that are fun, interactive and stimulating
- Emergency language sessions to support the learner in the first two to three days

- Opportunities for self-study and home learning through a 'Remember Book'
- Supporting the child's home language
- Visual, auditory and kinaesthetic learning
- Revision of recently learned English, which forms a key part of every lesson
- A supportive, daily learning routine
- Opportunities to make use of and develop communication strategies
- Cross-curricular links and opportunities for excursions
- Opportunities to practise the language through applying learning to real-life situations
- Creating a booklet about themselves as they work through the programme
- A wealth of carefully tailored, themed resources at the back of the book, including tips, worksheets and references to other good resources.

The programme has been made flexible through its approach to assessment, planning, teaching and learning in order to ensure that adaptation is made appropriately for EAL learners. The programme applies current thinking on EAL and good practice in learning and teaching in order to ensure that, 'every child succeeds within a culture of high expectations' (DfES, 2006b). It has been based on tried and tested research. The programme was first introduced in Lawdale Junior School in Tower Hamlets, London, and later used in other schools within the borough. It has since been revised in order to offer even more effective provision.

How it works – in practice

This is a 10-week programme which provides lessons and resources for an adult to teach English as an additional language to individuals or small groups of pupils. Learning is based on baseline assessment. If pupils have grasped the key learning, the programme will be shorter. Each week is called a 'unit'. It aims to be a week in length and is split into days: 1a = Monday, 1b = Tuesday and so on up to 1e. The teacher of the programme should use the baseline assessment (see Appendix 2) to decide which units to teach. At the end of each lesson, the teacher reassesses the pupils using the assessment for learning form (see Appendix 4). This informs future planning, which can be based around areas of difficulty identified in the assessment.

Teachers should use their judgement to keep the programme well-paced and progressive. There are a lot of activities included in each lesson that often take longer than the allocated time. In these cases, the teacher should select the activities which will motivate the learner and provide the best support for moving the children on quickly. The teacher can do this by editing the lesson plans or using the EAL optional planner, which is explained under 'Guidance on planning and teaching the programme' (see page 9; also see Appendices 6 and 7).

Before the programme commences, it is important that newcomers to English have some survival language. For this reason, six emergency language sessions have been included before the programme starts (see pages 21–25). It is advisable that these sessions are completed in the first three days of arrival. They are designed to provide each pupil with some key grammar and vocabulary that will allow them to function on a very basic level. The new learning provided in these lessons is revisited later in the programme in order to consolidate and provide more time to understand it in different contexts. It does not matter if the children do not grasp all of what is taught in the six sessions. It is designed to

relieve the stress of not being able to communicate.

Chapter 5 provides some useful resources to support children learning English as an additional language such as ideas and helpful reviews on good resources and ideas on forming an EAL resource box to support learning.

At the end of this programme, pupils should be proficient in the basics of English. However, this does not mean that they should be expected to achieve at the same level as their peers, but rather that the class teacher will be able to differentiate for the EAL learner more easily in mainstream lessons. The learners will also have a good foundation to build on in order to close the gap between themselves and their peers.

The Remember Book

'Opportunities should be provided for children to initiate their own learning and to use and apply the literacy skills they have been taught' (DfES, 2006b). These opportunities can be fostered through the use of a 'Remember Book' that forms a large part of the pupils' learning in this programme. A Remember Book is a notebook small enough to fit in a pocket (A6 size), but with enough space between the lines for pupils who know how to write to feel comfortable writing in them. Throughout the course, the pupils should write, update and revise new learning in the book in order to practise pronunciation, accuracy and understanding of new words and sentences.

The Remember Book has two functions.

1   To provide a record of what pupils have learned at the end of every lesson in order to support revision of English outside the class.

2   To record independent learning in order to provide opportunities for understanding new learning in lessons and then revising the new language outside the class.

The teacher should write the new learning for the lesson in advance and get the children to stick it in the front of their book during the lesson. It would be helpful to have the new language copied and ready for the children to stick into their Remember Books before the start of the lesson. Unless children are very able, it is better to cut and stick the new language instead of writing. This is because writing can be slow and inaccurate, especially with younger pupils or those in the early stages of learning.

Children must take their Remember Book and a pencil with them everywhere and be encouraged to write words or sentences in the back of the book as soon as they learn useful language. If children are literate in a home language, then they should be encouraged to write the translation. If not, they can draw a visual to remind them or just write the word on its own. It doesn't matter about spelling at this stage – it's the speaking, listening and remembering that is important. The attention to detail in the spelling can come later. Children use the back of the book to avoid making it messy and mixing up their useful, independently learnt words with the lesson work positioned at the front of the book.

Each page should be folded into two. For example:

Home language	English
_____	_____
_____	_____
_____	_____
_____	_____
	Page 1

Home language	English
_____	_____
_____	_____
_____	_____
_____	_____
	Page 2

Children can use the Remember Book independently by:

■   Adding new words at the back
■   Folding the page so they can't see the English and use their translations to look, cover, say and check that they remember the new word
■   Ticking off words they know and highlighting words they find difficult
■   Copying out the new learning on to post-it notes which they can stick on the wall and learn. These post-it notes could be stuck randomly around the house on specific objects as a label of what it is or put in key places where the children spend time; for example, next to the bed, by the TV or at the back of the front door.

Children can use the Remember Book with a parent or friend by:

■   The parent or friend reading the word in the home language and then the child saying it in English
■   The parent or friend reading the word in English and the child saying it in the home language
■   The child reading the words aloud for the parent or friend who can then check their pronunciation
■   The parent or friend giving the child five words a day from the book in the morning to be reviewed throughout the day.

The Remember Book should form part of the children's homework and can become part of the daily homework routine. The work they focus on in their Remember Book will ensure that they are surrounded by language in school and at home. This will motivate them, help them to identify what they need to learn and support progression.

Cross-curricular links

The *Primary Framework for Literacy and Mathematics Learning* (DfES, 2006b) outlined that, 'children learning EAL must be supported to access curriculum content . . . it is critical to maintain a level of cognitive challenge consistent with that of the rest of the class'. It is important to provide, 'opportunities to reinforce and enhance learning'. It states that, 'Literacy should be at the heart of the curriculum planning so that the subject matter from other curriculum areas is available as content or stimulus for speaking, listening, reading and writing.' Opportunities have therefore been provided for possible cross curricular links in order to practise and apply learning. It is important to consider the use of additional objectives so the children can know and use the language demanded by the curriculum.

Links have been made to various school subjects in order to offer some suggestions on how children can apply their learning and make it more 'real'. These links should only be used if a child has studied the previous units or if assessment shows that the child understands the grammar from the units leading up to the one concerned. For example, if the child does not understand the learning intentions for the grammar in units 1–5, it is not advisable to start at unit 6. It is important for the child to be continually successful and covering what might be too hard might mean we are setting children up to fail. Having said this, vocabulary can be learned at any time.

The programme can also be made cross-curricular through excursions. They are not only an opportunity to apply their new language in context, but also offer a rich learning experience and a chance for children to ask questions. This is especially important when some new arrivals may have never experienced day-to-day outings like this in their new country. An excursion offers another way of helping them acclimatise to their new environment.

Suggestions for excursions:

- Unit 8 – A supermarket to practise food, classifiers of quantity, countable and uncountable nouns and so on.
- Unit 9 – A café to practise making a request, I would like . . ., I don't understand, Do you have . . .?
- Unit 10 – A town to practise places and shops, directions, prepositions, Where is/are. . .?

If excursions are not an option then role play should be heavily integrated in learning.

A booklet about themselves

The children should make a booklet about themselves as part of the programme. The booklet is the product of the hard work the learners put into each unit and a reminder of what they have learnt. On completion, it can be presented to the class, displayed on the wall or taken home for a keepsake. It is developed during units 1 to 10 of the programme. After children have sat the baseline assessment, it may be obvious that they only need to touch on some of the first lessons or units. If this is the case, it may be a good idea to omit the making of the booklet entirely. However, if the teacher feels the booklet activity will be beneficial to a child's learning, and they do not want to complete the whole booklet, the child can make a stand alone page. It is likely that a child who arrives and can access most of this language will be able to make friends in English quickly and will have less of a need to produce such an item.

The pages of the booklet are displayed throughout the programme as necessary in order to provide examples of expectations. Before writing on any page of the booklet, pupils should complete a rough draft (to be written in their Literacy Books) and have this checked by their teacher or teaching assistant. Each page of the book must be completed to the pupil's best possible standard; for example, neat handwriting, neatly drawn coloured illustrations. If they can, they must also write the sentences underneath in their first language.

Reading

Although this induction programme incorporates some topic-based reading, it does not incorporate a guided reading session. It is advised that the class teacher provides beginners to English with daily guided reading opportunities. Guided readers provided in an EAL classroom resource box (see Chapter 5) are excellent as they are specifically geared towards children learning English (EAL-guided readers contain a limited number of carefully selected words written in basic tenses). There are also comprehension questions in the back of most of these books that would be helpful for the children to complete with some support. However, in many circumstances, a child's reading age will be so low that they may have to start on Foundation Stage level books.

It is also advised that you read to the children daily using basic stories with patterns and rhythm of language. Use one book per week, broken down as follows: day 1 – tell the story slowly, introducing vocabulary; day 2 – read the

story and ask the names of new vocabulary; day 3 – read the story and ask the child to read small, familiar parts with you; days 4 and 5 – you read, they read or read together.

Phonics

The Rose report (2006, quoted in DfES 2006b) identifies the 'importance of phonics as the prime approach to teaching word recognition for the vast majority of children, including those with EAL'. This programme does not include this and does assume some alphabetical and phonic knowledge is already understood by the child. Children new to English will benefit from a phonic programme if their home language does not have the same alphabet or phonic patterns as English. Even in languages with the same alphabet, be aware that the sounds of letters are often pronounced differently. It's therefore worth assessing and revising the child's phonic knowledge. For ages 7–9 there is usually access to a phonics revision programme within schools. However, For ages 9–11 phonics is not usually provided as, in most circumstances, children have acquired the skills. However, this is an exceptional circumstance and some provision must be made for the EAL learner. Speak to the person responsible for phonics so this can be organised within your school.

Guidance on planning and teaching the programme

This programme has been designed to make the teacher the expert. Teachers can make reference to the programme in order to enhance what they teach and adapt their planning and teaching so it is appropriate for the learner:

> Teachers are best placed to know how their children learn and will seek to create the best conditions for successful

language learning. In many cases this will involve approaches to teaching and learning with which they are familiar from good primary practice.

(DFES, 2005)

Before teaching each unit, you will need to refer to the baseline assessment (see page 14 and Appendices 2 and 3) to see if the unit's objectives are appropriate to the learner. If a learner answers the questions correctly (you may have to do some of this assessment verbally or add a few more examples to get a clear idea of what they know), then that learner already understands the objectives of the unit and needs to move to the next unit containing objectives that they do need to learn. The programme should be followed in numerical order. For example, the pupils may need to study units 2, 3, 5 and 6. It is fine to miss units 1 and 4 if they already understand, but it is not appropriate to study unit 6 before unit 2 as the pupils may not have understood the key concepts (covered in unit 2) in order to be successful in unit 6.

Teachers can use edited lesson plans or the EAL optional planner (see Appendix 6) for setting out their weekly lessons. The teacher will need an hour and a half at the beginning of every unit/week in order to plan and resource appropriately for the learner.

The programme has been designed to teach groups of new arrivals; however, it can be adapted to teach individuals. The lessons are split into sections as shown below.

Lesson breakdown	Explanation	Estimated timing (mins)
Review	This is a review of the preceding lesson. The teacher can plan for this by using the plenary or introduction from the previous lesson in order to recap or by sharing homework that revises this.	10
Teaching new language through speaking and listening	This part of the lesson is about teaching through speaking and listening. It introduces the learning intention so that the children know exactly what they are learning.	20
Independent learning	This part of the lesson is about practising and applying. The independent learning can be a speaking and listening, reading or writing activity. It may come in many forms (advised in each lesson) such as a game or matching activity. Often, the independent learning is focused around writing.	20
Extension	If children have successfully understood learning intentions in the independent learning, they can progress to the extension activity.	
Plenary and assessment for learning	The plenary is a chance to revisit learning and refer back to the learning intentions. It allows both the teacher and the child to assess the child's understanding of the learning intention. This	5

Lesson breakdown	Explanation	Estimated timing (mins)
	assessment should inform future learning. Nothing new should be introduced at this stage.	
Remember Book	The children must write down or stick the new learning in their Remember Book to revise at home and in future lessons.	5
Revision from previous lessons or their Remember Book	This short session could happen at a different time of the day from the main lesson. This is a revision of learning from previous lessons. Teachers can choose to revisit a plenary or introduction from a past lesson that children found difficult (based on the assessment for learning). The revision session may also involve sharing new words from their Remember Book.	15

Creating a successful lesson

Effective planning

The teacher should plan what will be taught. The planning will require an hour and a half at the beginning of every unit/week in order to look at a child's needs from their baseline assessment and assessment for learning form, then planning and resourcing can be decided upon accordingly. The baseline assessment and assessment for learning should inform learning intentions. Revision sections are included in the planning to allow you further consideration in consolidating areas of weakness.

Clear learning intentions

Make sure that the child knows exactly what they are learning to do. You need to be specific about the learning intention at the beginning, middle and end of the lesson. Stick to the objective and try not to deviate until you reach the revision section of the lesson. It can be useful to put the learning intention on the board at the start of every lesson and make it the title of the children's work. Then both you and the children will get used to this routine and always know exactly what you are trying to achieve. If children have useful questions unrelated to the learning intention, make a note of them and remember to use the revision session as a learning opportunity to revisit the question/s.

Revision for consolidation

Revision is important for consolidation of learning. Children should spend a large part of the lesson revising what they learned either in the preceding lesson or in previous lessons. This can be taken from their Remember Book, introductions or plenary from a previous lesson they enjoyed or found challenging. Do not be afraid to repeat.

If children haven't understood the learning intention and your assessments show that they need further support, adapt the resources to provide a scaffold for further learning. Don't be afraid to obtain resources from other books in order to recap and revise (there are plenty listed in Chapter 5).

Some units spend very little time on a learning intention. If further consolidation is needed, it can be built into the revision sessions. Use revision sessions wisely to cover what is not clearly understood or embedded.

The teacher is the best judge on whether the child needs further work on learning intentions and not the programme – the programme is a guide and not a dictation. Teachers must do whatever they can to support the learner in making good progress. They need to be flexible.

Patience

Learners need time to think. They may look blank for a while but just need time to process the new learning. Do not be tempted to answer for them. If you can see they can't answer, maybe a prompt would help them remember half of what they are learning. Remembering half is better than you giving them the whole new learning again. Obviously, do not labour a point. If they really don't understand, just be positive and give them the answer. Maybe you could say, 'We don't know that. We will do it again later. Have a good look at it so that you know next time.' Then come back to it at the end of the lesson.

Brain breaks for enhanced concentration

According to Smith and Call (2001), 'humans have natural attentional highs and lows throughout the day, which occur in cycles of between 90–110 minutes'. At different points in the cycle, the child, 'will be better at paying different types of attention'. They believe that 'chunking down tasks into smaller or manageable units allows diffusions or "downtime" where a different and additional form of learning takes place. The child stays engaged with learning but is perhaps allowed to do so through a different activity.' For this reason, brain breaks and changing of tasks are extremely important.

When lessons are long, use the natural breaks in the lesson format to do something that refreshes the children's concentration: ask them to have a glass of water; move them from the chairs to a carpet area; play a short, low key game; get them to put their hands on their head, then their shoulders, then ears, quickly and then slowly and so on. Providing some kind of appropriate distraction to help them refocus can be really effective.

Another idea is to use Brain Gym®, 'a program of physical movements that enhance learning and performance in all areas' (www.braingym. org). It was developed in the 1970s with the work of educators Dr Paul Dennison and Gail E. Dennison and has been successful worldwide.

Gestures for improved learning

The use of gestures in learning ensures teachers take advantage of the learning styles as follows (Marion, 2005):

- 'Auditory modality', which would be provided by the teacher's voice and the repetition
- 'Visual modality', which would be exposed through the visualisation of gestures
- 'Kinaesthetic modality', which would appear thanks to the reproduction of gestures.

Gestures are an exceptionally helpful way to secure children's understanding of new language. We assume,

> that the use of teacher's gestures in the learning of foreign vocabulary can have an effect on memorisation; but to make the most of this effect, teachers should make sure that the children reproduce the gestures while repeating the words. Thus, they will be more active in their repetition and reinforce its trace in memory.
> (Marion, 2005)

Children can take advantage of your gestures by copying what you say and your gesture. For example, in the first lesson you could say, 'Listen' and put your hand over your ear. At this point, the children can do the same and say, 'Listen'. Every time you say, 'Listen', you repeat the same gesture and the children copy. They will quickly understand the meaning of 'Listen' as they understand the gesture and will always hear the word when you put your hand over your ear. This is one way of ensuring children understand your instructions. However, gestures can also be used in this way with the taught vocabulary. For example, when teaching 'Swimming', you show with your arms that you are swimming and they can copy and say, 'Swimming'.

Getting pronunciation right from the start

At the beginning of every lesson, the new language is introduced through speaking and listening. This is the time to address children's pronunciation. You need to offer a clear model on how to pronounce the new language. Your model will support them in developing their words correctly. Pronunciation often goes uncorrected in the later stages of children learning a language. Poor pronunciation can mean words are indecipherable. By paying attention to pronunciation in the beginning, children can build on the foundation of sounds you provide which helps them to develop correctly in the future. If they are getting the pronunciation wrong, repeat the word slowly, breaking it down into syllables and repeating, then ask the children to repeat back. Avoid saying 'no' or 'that's wrong'. The children will know they are wrong when you say it again and ask them to repeat. They can then self-correct.

Using talk partners

During the programme, regular reference is made to children working in pairs in order to enhance their opportunities for speaking and listening independently. It may be useful to put children with a 'talk partner'. This can save time and gives the children security and enjoyment in knowing who they will work with each time you say, work in pairs.

Eliciting what they know

The programme provides a very structured way of presenting the new language and often assumes little to no knowledge of what is to be taught. However, as the children spend more time in their English-speaking environment, they will develop a wealth of grammar and vocabulary knowledge that we need to consider when teaching. Don't assume they don't know. If you can elicit what they know before providing them with the answers to new language, they will feel successful and motivated to learn more. You may be surprised that they do already know what you're going to teach and therefore you'll need to move on immediately. Consider this in your planning and teaching.

Dictionaries – friend or foe?

It is very easy for children to become reliant on dictionaries. They want to have an accurate answer and an accurate spelling, neither of which are always important. In the early stages of learning English, overusing dictionaries can be a barrier to progress as children quickly become bogged down with too many words that they cannot understand. Some children spend too much time looking at their dictionary and not on enough time practising the key new language. Other children haven't learned how to use one or haven't consolidated their alphabet so try their hardest with limited success. Obviously, there is a place for dictionaries, especially picture dictionaries, but under the right circumstances, and it is important not to let them 'take over' from the learning experience.

Assessment

Baseline and formative assessment underpins the programme, while assessment for learning is embedded in the programme. This is based on findings from research conducted by Black and Wiliam (1998). They identified that:

- Pupils need effective feedback
- Pupils need to be actively involved in their own learning
- Teachers need to take account of assessment in order to inform teaching
- Teachers have enormous influence on the motivation of pupils
- There is a need for pupils to assess themselves.

This was broken down further into:

- Sharing learning goals with pupils
- Involving pupils in self-assessment
- Providing feedback that leads to pupils recognising their next steps and how to take them
- Underpinning with confidence that every student can improve.

> (Assessment Reform Group, 1999, quoted in Clarke, 2001)

Baseline assessment

Each pupil needs to sit the baseline assessment (see Appendices 2 and 3) in order to help the teacher understand the children's needs. This assessment will allow the teacher to decide, first, if the programme would be suitable for the child and, second, how to place the child quickly and accurately on to the appropriate unit. Please be aware that children may not have seen an assessment like this and may not be able to answer the questions even though they understand the concept. Therefore, careful thought must be given to how and what assessment questions are to be verbally asked or explained. If the children do not complete all the questions in the assessment successfully, they can complete the units associated with the questions they got wrong.

Assessment for learning

At the end of every lesson, each pupil's understanding of the unit is assessed using an assessment for learning form, including key notes for informing future lessons added under the column 'Notes for future planning'. This, along with the teacher assessment on each child's performance during the lesson, will inform teacher planning. (The assessment forms are included in Appendix 4.) It is advisable to have the assessment for learning form with you in order to update it during or at the end of the lesson.

The assessment forms require the use of a triangle $\triangle$ to show the level of understanding each child has of the learning intention. A one-sided triangle next to the child's name would mean they don't understand and the new learning needs to be revisited. A two-sided triangle would mean they almost understand and may need a little more consolidation to fully grasp the concept. A fully drawn triangle would mean that the child understands the new learning and is ready to move on. This assessment for learning should be used to inform the revision sessions. The learning intentions children find difficult should be revisited regularly so that the learning is consolidated. Upon grasping the concept, the assessment record needs to be updated.

Any method could be used to collect this assessment information. For example:

- Observations
- Marking
- Questioning
- Pupil self-assessment.

Pupil self-assessment

It is strongly recommended that pupils self-assess their learning. If children are involved in assessing their needs, they can be actively involved on deciding what they need to learn next. Learners are then able to take ownership in applying themselves to new learning and reassessing themselves to see what progress they have made. Self-assessment is very motivating for children and helps them to take responsibility for their own learning.

Some methods of pupil self-assessment:

■ Ask pupils to show how much they understand the learning intention by showing their hand with a number of fingers that reflect how much they understand. For example, five fingers shows they understand, three fingers means they think they understand, no fingers means they don't understand.

■ Ask pupils to draw a face under the work they complete in their Remember Book or on the assessment for learning form that reflects how much they understand the learning intention. For example, a ☺ means they understand, a straight lined face 😐 means they think they understand, and ☹ means they do not understand.

■ Ask pupils to tell you how much they understand the learning intention. For example, I understand how to . . ., I think I understand how to . . ., or I don't understand how to. . . .

■ The pupils can use traffic light colours to signify understanding. For example, showing red means children don't understand, yellow/orange means they aren't sure and green means they understand.

■ Children can show thumbs up if they understand and thumbs down if they don't.

Whichever method is chosen can fit with the whole-school approach to pupil self-assessment.

Assessment using the Extended Scale for EAL learners

The assessment criteria for children with EAL in the National Curriculum is called the Extended Scale (see Appendix 5). It is an extension of the standard scale of assessment. It is used to make the first assessment of a pupil starting school as soon as it is reasonable to do so. The scale is then used at regular intervals until the pupil's work meets the relevant expectations of the National Curriculum levels. A good way to track the progress of the EAL learner is to highlight when they have achieved each objective on a half-termly basis using different colours and a date next to when each objective is achieved. Appendix 5 can be used for this and can follow the pupil across school years until they are accessing similar levels to their peers in English.

Success and praise

With regards to praise and encouragement, Clarke (2001) outlined that, 'the language of praise can have varying effects on children's self esteem and ability to be self evaluative and independent'. She outlined the importance of praise appropriate to a learning culture. 'Praise is like other forms of reward which discourage children from judging for themselves what is right and wrong. Praise may lead to dependency because children come to rely on the authority figure to tell them what is right or wrong, good or bad' (Kamii, 1984, quoted in Clarke, 2001). Clarke identifies research by Highscope (1995, quoted in Clarke, 2001) which suggests rewards can be related to the learning culture by acknowledging children's work with specific comments; for example, 'I notice you used a capital letter correctly, that's the first time I have seen you do this. It shows you understand how to use a capital letter.' Comments like these are far more effective than saying, 'Well done' with no reference to what was achieved. Another form of good practice is to, 'encourage children to describe their efforts, ideas and products by asking open ending questions – "What can you tell me about . . .?", "How did you . . .?", "I notice you've . . .", "What will you do next?" This gives them power to become self evaluative'.

It is also important for children to be successful, even if this means going slower or recapping again. If they are not successful, they will not be achieving, probably not be motivated and therefore not be keen to learn. Positive encouragements need to be used at every appropriate opportunity.

Use words such as:

- 'Try again.'
- 'You made a mistake, great, we can learn from this.'
- 'Good effort, have you looked at doing it this way?'

- 'If you can do . . . you're doing really well.' (Only say this if you know they can.)

Try to be specific with your praise by using words such as:

- 'I like the way you . . .'
- 'You made the mistake of . . . we can learn from this.'

If you want children to correct themselves, try not to use a negative comment. Instead, say: 'Try that again. Does it sound right?' If they can't say it, model it for them and then get them to do it. Model it again if they still can't do it. Do this until they CAN do it! Remember, they should be successful.

Avoid negativity. Stay away from words such as:

- 'No.'
- 'Wrong.'
- 'You didn't do this.'
- 'You forgot the . . .'

3

The programme

Overview: pre-induction sessions

Emergency language session 1

Vocabulary learning intention	Grammar learning intention
Hello, goodbye Thank you	My name is . . . What's your name? How are you? Fine, thank you.

Emergency language session 2

Vocabulary learning intention	Grammar learning intention
Yes, No Thank you Toilet Some water	Can I have some water please? Can I go to the toilet please?

Emergency language session 3

Vocabulary learning intention	Grammar learning intention
–	I don't understand. I understand. Can you say that again please?

Emergency language session 4

Vocabulary learning intention	Grammar learning intention
Pen, pencil, book, some water	What is this in English? Have you got . . .?

Emergency language session 5

Vocabulary learning intention	Grammar learning intention
Verbs, e.g. come, go, have, say	Present tense, e.g. I go home.

Emergency language session 6

Vocabulary learning intention	Grammar learning intention
Past tense verbs, e.g. came, went, had, said Future tense, e.g. will	Past tense, e.g. I went home. Future tense, e.g. I will go home.

Overview: units

Unit 1: Getting to know you

Vocabulary learning intention	Grammar learning intention	Possible cross-curricular links
Hello, goodbye Spelling their name Countries/place names Yes, No Numbers 1–11 Alphabet Colours	What's your name? My name is . . . How old are you? I am ___ years old. I live in . . . I come from . . . Is this blue? Yes, it is/No, it isn't. Full stop Capital letter Question mark	Geography – countries, the home, connecting to world Maths – counting to 11 Literacy – letter writing, e.g. introducing yourself Science – investigations, e.g. Is this blue? Art – colours, self portraits

Unit 2: What's this in English?

Vocabulary learning intention	Grammar learning intention	Possible cross-curricular links
Classroom vocabulary, e.g. pen, pencil, ruler, table Belongs to I don't know Numbers 1–50 About Friend Add Subtract Vowels	What's this/that in English? (What is) What's this? What's that? It's a . . ./ It isn't a . . . a/an + the (vowel + an) Possessive adjectives, e.g. your, my Possessive ('s), e.g. Whose . . . is this? This is . . .'s pen.	Maths – addition, subtraction, counting 1–50 Literacy – reports, e.g. It's a . . . Art – objects and meaning, still life drawing, sculpture, e.g. classroom objects

Unit 3: I like Literacy

Vocabulary learning intention	Grammar learning intention	Possible cross-curricular links
School subjects Verb Pronoun	What's this subject? General sentence structure, e.g. subject, verb, object (I drink milk) I like . . ./I don't like . . . Present simple, third person, e.g. I walk/he walks	Literacy – fact, e.g. The cat drinks milk, and opinion, e.g. I don't like cheese. Report writing, e.g. The animal eats meat.

Unit 4: My favourite animal is a cat

Vocabulary learning intention	Grammar learning intention	Possible cross-curricular links
Animals Imperatives/classroom instructions, e.g. turn light off, close door, mind the, be careful, stand up My favourite . . .	a/an Plurals s/es/ies/ves This, that, these, those What are these/those?	Science – habitats Literacy – report writing, e.g. The animal eats meat. Instructions Physical Education – imperatives

Unit 5: Have you got any brothers and sisters?

Vocabulary learning intention	Grammar learning intention	Possible cross-curricular links
Family Description	Have you got . . .?/Has she got . . .? I have got/I haven't got (I've got) He has got/She hasn't got (He's got) Who is this? This is . . . She's my friend Possessive adjectives (your, my, her, his), -'s	Literacy – describing characters Art – portraits, portraying relationships

Unit 6: I like football

Vocabulary learning intention	Grammar learning intention	Possible cross-curricular links

Hobbies
Sport
Ordinal numbers
  (first, second, third)
	Can/can't (cannot)
	Likes/dislikes, e.g. Do you like . . .?
	  Yes, I do/No, he doesn't (does not).
		Physical Education – sports
		Maths – ordinal numbers
		Literacy – self-assessment
		  'can do' statements

Unit 7: Have you got any sugar?

Vocabulary learning intention	Grammar learning intention	Possible cross-curricular links

Food	Countable/uncountable nouns
	Classifiers, e.g. a pack of, a bottle of
	Some/any
	Have you got any/some?
	How much/many have you got?
	I have got . . .
		Science – healthy eating,
		  teeth and eating
		Maths – measuring
		Design and Technology –
		  packaging, making
		  sandwiches, bread

Unit 8: There is a shower in the bathroom

Vocabulary learning intention	Grammar learning intention	Possible cross-curricular links

Home	There is/There are
	There isn't any
	There aren't any
	Are there/Is there . . .?
	Yes, there is/No, there isn't (is not).
	Prepositions, e.g. in, on, under, next
	  to, behind, in front of, near,
	  between
		Geography – home/local area
		Science – questioning, e.g.
		  Are there . . .?
		Maths – describing
		  position
		Art – viewpoint
		Design and Technology –
		  shelters

Unit 9: Can I have a glass of water please?

Vocabulary learning intention	Grammar learning intention	Possible cross-curricular links
Sorry I don't understand Please Thank you Pardon Food Waiter Restaurant Excuse me Feelings, e.g. thirsty, hungry, hot	Making a request, e.g. I would like . . .? Here you are. Anything else? Do you have . . .? Yes, I do/No, I don't. Can I have . . .? Yes, you can/No, you can't. Please can I go to the toilet? Do you/Does he? Yes, he does/No, you don't. I want . . .	Science – healthy eating, keeping healthy Literacy – dialogues, plays

Unit 10: Where is the library?

Vocabulary learning intention	Grammar learning intention	Possible cross-curricular links
Shops/places Directions, e.g. turn left, turn right, straight on	Where is/are the . . .? Prepositions, e.g. in, on, under, next to, behind, in front of, near, between	Maths – position and direction Geography – local area, contrasting locality Art – picture this History – different settlements

Please be aware that resource sheets to support the programme can be found in Appendix 8. The following will also be required for every lesson: Literacy Book, Remember Book, whiteboard and pens.

Pre-induction: emergency language sessions

Pre-induction can be broken down into six small sessions and should be covered in the first three days. It is emergency language designed to give each pupil some key grammar and vocabulary which will allow them to function on a very basic level. The new learning provided in this lesson is revisited later in the programme in order to revise and to provide time to understand it in different contexts. It does not matter if the pupils do not grasp everything in the six sessions, as long as they can converse enough to relieve the stress of being unable to make themselves understood.

Vocabulary learning intention

- Hello, goodbye
- Yes, No

- Thank you
- Pen
- Pencil
- Book (Remember Book)
- Toilet
- Some water

Grammar learning intention

- My name is . . . What's your name?
- How are you? Fine, thank you.
- Can I have some water please?
- Can I go to the toilet please?
- I don't understand.
- I understand.
- Can you say that again please?
- What is this in English?
- Have you got . . .?
- I go home. I went home. I will go home.
- I have some water. I had some water. I will have some water.
- I say hello. I said hello. I will say hello.

Resources

- New language ready to stick in their Remember Book
- Remember Book template
- Glass of water
- Mini whiteboard and pen

SESSION 1

My name is . . . What's your name?

Introduce yourself, e.g. 'My name is . . .' and write this on the board. Say 'What's your name?' and invite each pupil to answer individually, 'My name is . . .'. Write all their names on the board. Write, 'What's your name?' on the board. Each child asks another child, 'What's your name?' and the other child answers 'My name is . . .'.

Give out the Remember Book and show the pupils where to fold the page. Then show

them where to put the English and where to write their home language or picture (have an example ready to show them). Ask the pupils to stick the new language into their Remember Book.

Hello, how are you?
Fine, thank you.
Goodbye.

Write the following vocabulary on the board and ask them to repeat it:

> Hello, how are you?
> Fine, thank you.
> Goodbye.

Leave the room and come in and say 'Hello, how are you?' and shake one child's hand. Say 'Fine, thank you' and ask them to repeat it. Then leave the room and say, 'Goodbye' and wave. Do this again and expect them to answer 'Fine, thank you' without your prompt (point at the words on the board if they aren't sure what to say or prompt them by whispering to them). Then ask each child to come into the room, shake another child's hand and say 'Hello, how are you?' The child they chose must say 'Fine, thank you', then they walk out of the room and say 'Goodbye' and wave. Ask the pupils to stick the new language into their Remember Book.

SESSION 2

Can I have some water please? Yes. Thank you.

Write on the board:

> Can I have some water please?
> Yes.
> Thank you.

Read together 'some water' and point to the glass of water and say 'some water'. Underline 'some water'. Give one child a glass of water and say 'Can I have some water please?' and signal for them to give this to you and say 'Yes'. Take the offered water and say 'Thank you'. Do this again and again with different pupils. Then get another child to ask you for some water. Ask the pupils to ask each other for the water. Ask the pupils to stick the new language into their Remember Book.

Can I go to the toilet please? Yes/No.

Take all the pupils to the toilet. Go inside. Point to the toilet and say 'toilet'. Walk outside the toilet door together. Say 'Can I go to the toilet please?' Write this on the mini whiteboard. Show the answers 'Yes' and 'No'. Get each child to repeat the sentence and then role play them coming to you to ask if they can go to the toilet. They can only go inside if you say 'Yes'. Ask the pupils to stick the new language into their Remember Book.

SESSION 3

I don't understand.
I understand.
Can you say that again please?

Draw a stick man on the board with a question mark over his head and scratching his head. Then shrug your shoulders, scratch your head and look confused. Say 'I don't understand' and write it on the board. Ask the pupils to do the same and say 'I don't understand'. Ask them a question, speaking quickly so that they are unlikely to know what you mean. Then look at them and point to the board. Ask them to shrug their shoulders and say 'I don't understand'. Write on the board, 'Can you say that again please?' Ask them to repeat after you 'Can you say that again please?'

Leave the room and come back in and ask them the question again. Ask them to say 'Can

you say that again please?' Repeat the question equally quickly. Next, point to the sentence again to indicate for them to ask you again, 'Can you say that again please?' You then say it again. Then point to, 'I don't understand' and ask them to say this and shrug their shoulders. Pupils practise together.

Ask them really quickly, 'Can I have some water please?' When a child asks you 'Can you say that again please?' say it slower so that they understand and pass you the water. Write on the board and nod 'I understand'. Ask them to repeat.

Ask the pupils to stick the new language into their Remember Book.

SESSION 4

What is this in English?
Pen, pencil, book, some water

Write 'What is this in English?' on the board. Ask pupils to say this after you again and again. Then you point and they say the sentence without you telling them how to say it. Give one of them a pencil and point to the sentence for them to say 'What is this in English?' You then say 'It's a pencil'. Each child in turn then picks or points to any object in the room and says 'What's this in English?' and you answer accordingly.

Ask the pupils to stick the new language into their Remember Book.

Have you got . . .?

Choose three objects the pupils learned from the previous sessions such as a pen, a pencil, some water, a Remember Book. Put them in the middle of the table. Ensure the pupils are using a/an/some with the noun, e.g. a pen, an apron, some water. (There is no need to explain why at this stage but they need to use them for their sentence to be correct. This topic is covered in the early sessions of the induction programme.)

Write on the board: 'Have you got . . .? Yes/No.' Say to one child, 'Have you got a pencil?' Ask the child to say 'Yes' or 'No'. Repeat this activity with a number of different objects.

Take the objects and put them in a bag. Leave one out secretly. The pupils have to guess which one is left out by asking you questions using 'Have you got . . .?'

Ask the pupils to stick the new language into their Remember Book.

SESSION 5

I go home.
I come to school.
I have some water.
I say hello.

Resources

- Pictures of your school
- Picture of a home (you could use resource sheet 8a)

Write on the board:

> go
> come
> have
> say

Ask the pupils to 'Go home' (do this by waving your hand for them to go away from you and stand next to a picture of the home) and point to the word 'go' and ask them to repeat.

Ask the pupils to come to you and to 'Come to school' (do this by waving your hand for them to come to the picture of the school) and point to 'come' and ask them to repeat.

Ask the pupils to 'have' some water (they can mime this or use real glasses of water). Point to the word 'have' and ask them to repeat.

Ask the pupils to 'say' hello (you can mime this first and they can copy) and point to the word 'say' and ask them to repeat.

Repeat these activities until the pupils can show and tell you what the verbs mean without your help. Ask individual pupils to say the verb instead of you and the rest of the pupils can follow the activity.

Write:

> I go home. (Draw a picture of a house to show home.)

> I come to school. (Use the school name so the pupils understand the word 'school'.)

> I have some water. (Drink some water to demonstrate this.)

> I say hello. (Say 'hello' to demonstrate this.)

Ask the pupils to say the sentences to each other and follow the actions accordingly.

SESSION 6

I went home.
I came to school.
I had some water.
I said hello.

I will go home.
I will come to school.

I will have some water.
I will say hello.

Resources

- Pictures of your school
- Picture of a home (you could use resource sheet 8a)

Ask one child to 'Go home' (do this by waving your hand for them to go away from you and stand next to a picture of the home in the same way as the previous session). Then ask them to sit down.

Write on the board: 'I went home.'

Do the same with each of the sentences. Showing the ideas of the child doing the action in the present and then in the past.

Write on the board: 'I will go home.'

Say the sentence then nod at a child to show you would like them to 'go home'. Make sure there is a gap between you giving this instruction and them doing it in order to show the future tense. Do the same with each of the sentences using 'will'.

Show on the board:

Past	←——— Present (now) ———→	Future
I went home.	I go home.	I will go home.
I came to school.	I come to school.	I will come to school.
I had some water.	I have some water.	I will have some water.
I said hello.	I say hello.	I will say hello.

You model one of the sentences. For example:

Present: Do the action and say 'I go home' as you do this.

Past: Do the action then sit down and say 'I went home'.

Future: Say the sentence 'I will go home' and then complete the action.

Repeat this yourself and then ask each child to say one sentence in past, present and future.

Getting to know you

Vocabulary learning intention

- Hello, goodbye
- Spelling their name
- Countries/place names
- Yes, No
- Numbers 1–11
- Alphabet
- Colours

Grammar learning intention

- What's your name? My name is . . .
- How old are you? I am __ years old.
- I live in . . .
- I come from . . .
- Is this blue? Yes, it is/No, it isn't (is not).
- Full stop
- Capital letter
- Question mark

Resources

- New language ready to stick in pupils' Remember Books
- Characters (the Scott family) – resource sheet 1a1
- Characters (the Matthew family) – resource sheet 1a2
- Characters (the residents of Torrington Town) – resource sheet 1a3
- Torrington Town – resource sheet 10b
- Card
- A4 paper
- Ball
- Example Personal Book
- Template for writing
- Literacy books
- Number cards 1–10
- Counters
- Globe
- Atlases
- Photocopied page of world
- Alphabet jigsaw – resource sheet 1d
- Alphabet picture (a–z with corresponding pictures)
- Book (any familiar book you have read together)
- Colours poster – resource sheet 1c
- Colour pencils

Lesson 1A

Vocabulary learning intention

- Hello, goodbye
- My name is
- Spelling their name
- This is . . .

Grammar learning intention

- What's your name? My name is . . .

Resources

- New language ready to stick in pupils' Remember Books
- Characters (the Scott family) – resource sheet 1a1
- Characters (the Matthew family) – resource sheet 1a2
- Characters (the residents of Torrington Town) – resource sheet 1a3
- Card
- A4 paper
- Ball
- Example Personal Book
- Template for writing

Teaching new language through speaking and listening

Introduce yourself 'My name is . . .' and write it on the board. Say 'What's your name?' and invite each pupil to answer individually 'My name is . . .'. Write all the pupils' names on the board.

Get the class to sit in a circle and you roll a ball to a pupil saying 'Hello, my name is . . . What's your name?' and ask the pupil to roll the ball back. Then roll the ball to another pupil. In turn, each pupil rolls the ball to someone else in the circle introducing themselves and asking other pupils their names.

When they have done this twice, change the rules slightly. They have to now say, 'Hello, my name is . . . This is . . .' and roll the ball to the person they introduce. Do this until they have remembered all the names.

Independent learning: pupils write these sentences in their Literacy Books.

Pupils start to create a Personal Book that contains details about themselves, their family and friends that they will add to throughout the lessons.

Personal Book, pages 1 and 2: pupils should write 'Hello, my name is . . . This is . . .'. Start on page 1 by writing 'My name is . . .' and ask them to draw a picture of themselves. Use a speech bubble to have them saying 'Hello'.

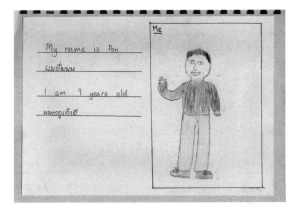 

On the next page, pupils write 'This is . . .'. Pupils write their friend's name and draw a picture of the friend. Make sure that they present this to the best of their ability. (Wherever possible, pupils should be encouraged to say and/or write the new learning in their home language.)

Use the characters on resource sheets 1a1 and 1a2 to say, 'What is her name? Her name is . . .' 'What is his name? His name is . . .' 'What is its name? Its name is . . .' This is a good chance for them to familiarise themselves with the characters on resource sheets 1a1 and 1a2. You can also refer to resource sheet 1a3 to give you an added understanding of each of the characters – this is for your reference and not for the pupils. The pupils will learn more about the characters as they progress through the programme.

Extension

Pupils write questions about the characters using, 'What is her name? It is . . . What is his name? It is . . . What is its name? Its name is . . .'

Plenary

Share their work. Look at the characters on resource sheets 1a1 and 1a2. Ask the pupils the characters' names using 'What's her/his/its name?'

Ask the pupils to stick the new language into their Remember Book.

Write 'Goodbye' on the board. Say 'Goodbye' at the end of class.

Ensure that you assess each pupil on their achievement of the vocabulary and grammar learning intentions using the assessment for learning form.

Lesson 1B

Vocabulary learning intention

■ Numbers 1–11

Grammar learning intention

■ How old are you? I am __ years old.

Resources

■ New language ready to stick in pupils' Remember Books
■ Characters – resource sheet 1a1
■ Characters – resource sheet 1a2
■ Number cards
■ Counters
■ Card
■ A4 paper

Review

Always revise learning from the preceding lesson before introducing new learning. Use the plenary or introduction from the previous lesson in order to recap.

Teaching new language through speaking and listening

Arrange numbers in a line from 1 to 11. Point to each number in turn. Say 'one' and point to the number 1. Pupils then repeat after you. Write the number in words underneath and add one dot to show what 1 is. Pupils use counters to count one at a time. Repeat for each number from 1 to 11 three times.

Try again and miss out some numbers. Pupils to try to remember the numbers you left out. Try again and again leaving different numbers out each time until the pupils remember all the numbers from 1 to 11.

Ask the pupils to write down the numeral, the number in words and the correct number of dots in their Literacy Books. For example:

1 one ●   2 two ●●

Leave two pages so they can come back later and add more numbers.

Write on the board 'How old are you?' Ask each child to answer: 'I am ___ years old.' Write their ages on the board. Ask them to sit in a line and say 'I am ___ years old. How old are you?' and the next child in the line answers 'I am ___ years old. How old are you?' to the next child and so on.

Independent learning: write on the board 'She is ___ years old. He is ___ years old.' Then ask pupils to say 'She/he is ___ years old. I am ___ years old.' Pupils write this in their Literacy Books.

Personal Book, pages 1 and 2: add to the bottom of page 1 'I am ___ years old.' And to the bottom of page 2 'She/he is ___ years old.'

Look at the characters on resource sheets 1a1 and 1a2. Ask 'How old is he/she/it?' (Wherever possible, pupils should be encouraged to say and/or write the new learning in their home language.)

Extension

Pupils write questions and answers about the characters using, 'How old is he/she/it?'

Plenary

Ask one child to point to a character and ask 'How old is he/she/it?' or 'How old are you?' and another to answer accordingly.

Ask the pupils to stick the new language into their Remember Book.

Ensure that you assess each pupil on their achievement of the vocabulary and grammar learning intentions using the assessment for learning form.

Lesson 1C

Vocabulary learning intention

- Countries/place names, e.g. Bangladesh, Somalia, England, Egypt, London

Grammar learning intention

- I live in . . .
- I come from . . .

Resources

- New language ready to stick in pupils' Remember Books
- Globe
- Atlases
- Copied page of world
- Card
- A4 paper
- Characters – resource sheet 1a1
- Characters – resource sheet 1a2
- Torrington Town – resource sheet 10b

Review

Always revise learning from the preceding lesson before introducing new learning. Use the plenary or introduction from the previous lesson in order to recap.

Teaching new language through speaking and listening

Look at an atlas and ask each child to find the country in which they are learning English. Write 'I live in . . .' (specify where) on the board. You read, they repeat. Now ask each child to say where they come from. Write 'I come from . . .' on the board. You read, they repeat. Now ask each child to try to find the country they come from on the atlas.

Independent learning: pupils write 'I come from . . .' and 'I live in . . .' (specify where) and describe where their friend comes from, e.g. 'He/she comes from . . .' in their Literacy Books.

Personal Book, page 3: stick a map of the world on to page 3. Pupils put a cross where they live and where they have come from and label, e.g. 'I come from Thailand. I live in . . .' (specify where). If they have time, they should also mark where their friend lives and comes from (the person they have drawn on page 2). (Wherever possible, pupils should be encouraged to say and/or write the new learning in their home language.)

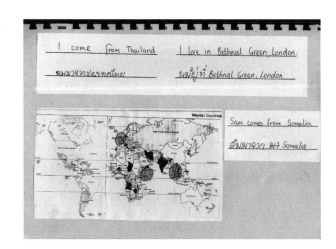

Extension

Use: 'He/she/they/we come from . . .' and 'He/she/they/we live in . . .' to describe their friends.

Plenary

Look at the characters on resource sheets 1a1 and 1a2. Say, 'They come from Torrington Town' and show the street map – resource sheet 10b. Ask the pupils to ask each other where they come from.

Ask the pupils to stick the new language into their Remember Book.

Ensure that you assess each pupil on their achievement of the vocabulary and grammar learning intentions using the assessment for learning form.

Revision

Revise learning from previous lessons by choosing a plenary or introduction from a past lesson that pupils found difficult or focus on learning from the Remember Books.

Lesson 1D

Vocabulary learning intention

- Alphabet

Grammar learning intention

- Full stop
- Capital letter
- Question mark

Resources

- New language ready to stick in pupils' Remember Books

- Alphabet jigsaw – resource sheet 1b
- Alphabet picture (a–z with corresponding pictures)
- Book (any familiar book you have read together)

Review

Always revise learning from the preceding lesson before introducing new learning. Use the plenary or introduction from the previous lesson in order to recap.

Teaching new language through speaking and listening

Arrange the alphabet in a line from a to z. Point to each letter in turn. You say the sound 'a' and point to 'a'. Pupils repeat. Say the name of a word that goes with an alphabet picture, pupils repeat after you. Repeat three times.

Write the letters of the alphabet in lower case in the air. Then write the letters in correct formation using a teacher model or handwriting chart. Pupils write down the alphabet in lower case in their Literacy Books.

Write on the board: 'capital letter', 'full stop' and 'question mark'. Look at a book (a basic book the pupils are familiar with) and point out the capital letters at the beginning of sentences and the full stop at the end. Say 'capital letter' and point, 'full stop' and point, 'question mark' and point. Read the section of the text and point to the capitals, full stops and question marks as you read in order to draw attention to them. Make sure you stop a little longer than usual at the full stop in order to emphasise its meaning.

You write the capital letters on the board and then use them as a template for writing them in the air. This will get the pupils used to writing the letters correctly before they put them down on paper. Then write the letters in correct formation using a teacher model or handwriting chart. Pupils write down the capitals in their Literacy Books. (Wherever possible, pupils should be encouraged to say and/or write the new learning in their home language.)

Independent learning: pupils make the alphabet jigsaw together. Please note: depending on the pupils' current understanding of the alphabet they could take a considerable amount of time to learn this. Consider covering the alphabet as part of a separate phonics programme.

Extension

Try to think of other words the pupils know that start with different letters of the alphabet. Teacher scribes, pupils copy the word next to the correct letter in the alphabet.

Plenary

Repeat the alphabet.

Ask the pupils to stick the new language into their Remember Book.

> **Ensure that you assess each pupil on their achievement of the vocabulary and grammar learning intentions using the assessment for learning form.**

Revision

Revise learning from previous lessons by choosing a plenary or introduction from a past lesson that pupils found difficult or focus on learning from the Remember Books.

Lesson 1E

Vocabulary learning intention

■ Colours: blue, green, red, black, pink, orange, brown, yellow, grey, purple, white

Grammar learning intention

■ Is it . . .? Yes, it is/No, it isn't.

Resources

■ New language ready to stick in pupils' Remember Books

■ Colour pencils
■ Colours poster – resource sheet 1c

Review

Always revise learning from the preceding lesson before introducing new learning. Use the plenary or introduction from the previous lesson in order to recap.

Teaching new language through speaking and listening

Show each colour pencil and say the colour (show the colour poster). Then write the colour on the board. Say again and they repeat. Repeat again together and ask the pupils to remember the colours.

Write on the board 'Is this blue?' and show a blue pencil. Then write 'Yes, it is' (nod your head). Pupils repeat. Then hold the blue pencil up and say 'Is this red?' and write on the board saying 'No, it isn't' and 'No, it is not' (shake your head). Try the same with the other colours and ask the pupils to answer 'Yes, it is' and 'No, it isn't'.

A pupil then holds up a pencil and asks 'Is this . . . (yellow)?' The others answer 'Yes, it is' or 'No, it isn't'.

Independent learning: pupils write the title 'colours' in their Literacy Books and then write the names of the colours and draw an associated coloured dot next to it.

Extension

Repeat the above using the following: cream, lilac, beige, dark, light.

Plenary

Point to colours in the classroom using the same vocabulary, 'Is this blue?' Pupils answer 'Yes, it is' or 'No, it isn't'. A child then does the same using colours in the room.

Ask the pupils to stick the new language into their Remember Book.

Ensure that you assess each pupil on their achievement of the vocabulary and grammar learning intentions using the assessment for learning form.

Revision

Revise learning from previous lessons by choosing a plenary or introduction from a past lesson that pupils found difficult or focus on learning from the Remember Books.

What's this in English?

Vocabulary learning intention

- Classroom vocabulary, e.g. pen, pencil, ruler, table
- Belongs to
- I don't know
- Numbers 1–50
- About
- Friend
- Add
- Subtract
- Vowels

Grammar learning intention

- What's this/that in English? (What is)
- What's this? What's that? It's a . . ./It isn't a . . .

- a/an + the (vowel + an)
- Possessive adjectives, e.g. your, my
- Possessives ('s)
- Whose . . . is this? This is . . .'s pen.

Resources

- New language ready to stick in pupils' Remember Books
- Visual labels for classroom – resource sheet 2a
- Blank labels
- Number line 1–50
- Numbers 1–100 – resource sheet 2b
- Characters – resource sheets 1a1 and 1a2
- Counters

Lesson 2A

Vocabulary learning intention

- Vowels – a, e, i, o, u
- Classroom vocabulary: nouns, e.g. pen, pencil, rubber, paper, notebook, glue, whiteboard, board, scissors, table, chair, drawer, bookshelf, wall, floor, door, window, ceiling, ruler

Grammar learning intention

- a/an

Key vocabulary: noun

- A noun is the name of a thing or a person, e.g. elephant, apple, house or Caroline.

Grammar rule: a/an

- We use 'an' before singular (i.e. not plural) nouns that start with a vowel sound (a, e, i, o, u), e.g. an elephant.
- We use 'a' before singular nouns that do not start with a vowel sound, e.g. a banana.

35

Resources

■ New language ready to stick in pupils' Remember Books

■ Visual labels for classroom – resource sheet 2a

■ Blank labels

Review

Always revise learning from the preceding lesson before introducing new learning. Use the plenary or introduction from the previous lesson in order to recap.

Teaching new language through speaking and listening

Write the word 'noun' and some examples. Pupils think of as many nouns as they can. If they don't know any, point to some. Show that a noun is something that can be touched.

Independent learning: write the title 'Vowel' on the board, say the word and pupils repeat. Write 'a, e, i, o, u' on the board, say the letter sounds and pupils repeat. Show that if a noun starts with a vowel, then 'an' must be put before it, e.g. an umbrella, an elephant. Nouns not starting a with vowel sound use 'a', e.g. a pen, a rubber. Nouns starting with a vowel sound use 'an', e.g. an envelope. Label some items. Pupils put 'a' or 'an' in front of their chosen nouns. Write down ten nouns with 'a' or 'an' before them. (Wherever possible, pupils should be encouraged to say and/or write the new learning in their home language.)

Extension

Identify further classroom vocabulary, e.g. paint brush, mirror, pin board.

Plenary

Say and write down a noun and pupils say if it's 'a' or 'an'.

Ask the pupils to stick the new language into their Remember Book.

Ensure that you assess each pupil on their achievement of the vocabulary and grammar learning intentions using the assessment for learning form.

Revision

Revise learning from previous lessons by choosing a plenary or introduction from a past lesson that pupils found difficult or focus on learning from the Remember Books.

Lesson 2B

Vocabulary learning intention

■ Classroom vocabulary, e.g. pen, pencil, rubber, glue, whiteboard, board, scissors, table, chair, drawer, bookshelf, wall, floor, door, window, ceiling, ruler

Grammar learning intention

■ What's this/that?
■ What's this/that in English?
■ It's a/an

Grammar rule: What's this/that? It's . . .

■ 'What's this?' is the same as saying 'What is this?'
■ We use 'What is this?' for a singular noun that is near, e.g. 'You can have this pencil' (said as you give the pencil to a person).
■ 'What's that?' is the same as saying 'What is that?'
■ We use 'What is that?' for a singular noun that is further away, e.g. 'You can have that book' (said as you point to a book on the shelf on the other side of the room).
■ 'It's . . .' is the same as saying 'It is . . .'.

Grammar rule: What are these/those?

■ We use 'these' to talk about plural nouns that are near, e.g. 'You can have these keys' (said as you give the keys to a pupil).
■ We use 'those' to talk about plural nouns that are further away, e.g. 'You can have those books' (said as you point to the bookshelf on the other side of the room).

Resources

■ New language ready to stick in pupils' Remember Books
■ Classroom items
■ Flip chart

Review

Always revise learning from the preceding lesson before introducing new learning. Use the plenary or introduction from the previous lesson in order to recap.

Teaching new language through speaking and listening

Ask 'What is this in English?' Write this sentence on the board and point to a pen in your hand. Then write 'It is a pen' on the board. Write the short versions 'What's this in English?' 'What's this?' and then 'It's a pen'. Ask individual pupils to point to objects they have near them and say 'What's this in English?' or 'What's this?' Other pupils can answer if they know and you write the answers on the board.

Point to something far away and say 'What's that in English?' or 'What's that?' Do this again and mix it with pointing to something near you saying 'What's this in English?' until pupils understand the difference between 'this' and 'that'.

Ask them to play a game: choose a child to say 'What's this in English?' or 'What's that in English?' whilst pointing. Class answers.

Independent learning: pupils write 'What's this in English? What's that in English?' as the title in their Literacy Books. They then write down the objects they have learned and draw a picture to go with them, e.g. It's a pen, It's a book. (Wherever possible, pupils should be encouraged to say and/or write the new learning in their home language.)

Poster: if there is time when they have finished, pupils can work in groups. Use a flip chart for each group and write the title 'Classroom vocabulary' in the middle of the page. Then ask the pupils to select the classroom vocabulary they have learned around the outside. Pupils can draw pictures to go with the words.

Extension

Use 'What are these/those?' in a similar way to identify plural objects near and far away.

Plenary

You say the vocabulary, pupils point to the label.

Ask the pupils to stick the new language into their Remember Books.

Ensure that you assess each pupil on their achievement of the vocabulary and grammar learning intentions using the assessment for learning form.

Revision

Revise learning from previous lessons by choosing a plenary or introduction from a past lesson that pupils found difficult or focus on learning from the Remember Books.

Lesson 2C

Vocabulary learning intention

- Classroom vocabulary
- Belongs to

Grammar learning intention

- Possessive adjectives, e.g. your, my, her, his
- The

Grammar rule: possessive adjectives

- We use possessive adjectives, e.g. your, my, her, his, to say who the noun belongs to. They are placed before the noun, e.g. your pen.

Grammar rule: the

- We use 'the' when we know exactly what person or thing we are talking about, e.g. look at the trousers.

Resources

- New language ready to stick in pupils' Remember Books

- Characters – resource sheet 1a1
- Classroom items

Review

Always revise learning from the preceding lesson before introducing new learning. Use the plenary or introduction from the previous lesson in order to recap.

Teaching new language through speaking and listening

Write on the board and say 'This is my pen' and show your pen. Write 'It belongs to me' and point to yourself. Then write and say 'This is your pen' and write 'It belongs to you' and point to the pupil's pen. Underline, 'my' and point to yourself. Underline 'your' and point to them. Go round the class and each pupil points and says 'This is my ___' and 'This is your ___'.

Split the class in half. Write 'This is his pen'. Show the characters from resource sheet 1a1 and draw a pen next to Edd and say, 'This is his pen' and then a pen next to Caroline and say, 'This is her pen'.

Ensure each child has an item of their own. Sit in one group, take a child's pen and say again, 'This is your pen' and give it back. Then go and get an item from the other group and say to the pupils in your group 'This is her/his ___'. Then go and give it back. Ask the pupils to practise doing the same.

Try again, take a girl's pen again and say 'This is her pen'. Write on the board 'a pen' and cross out the 'a' and write 'the' (we know which pen this is so we call it 'the pen' and not 'a pen'). Show some more examples with other pupils' pencils, rubbers and so on. Then pick up any random item they know the name of and say 'a ___' in order to emphasise the difference.

Independent learning: write 'This is my pen' and draw a picture of it. Write 'The pen belongs to ___' and 'This is your ___' then draw a picture of it. Write 'The ___ belongs to the teacher'. 'This is his ___' and draw a picture of it and write 'It belongs to ___ (a boy)'. 'This is her ___' and draw a picture and write 'It belongs to ___ (a girl)'. Pupils complete their own version. (Wherever possible, pupils should be encouraged to say and/or write the new learning in their home language.)

Extension

Introduce 'their' and/or 'our' in a similar manner.

Plenary

Pick up two more items and make statements, e.g. This is ___ pen.

Extension

Use resource sheet 1a1 to say, 'This is their cat', 'This is their baby'.

Ask the pupils to stick the new language into their Remember Books.

Ensure that you assess each pupil on their achievement of the vocabulary and grammar learning intentions using the assessment for learning form.

Revision

Revise learning from previous lessons by choosing a plenary or introduction from a past lesson that pupils found difficult or focus on learning from the Remember Books.

Lesson 2D

Vocabulary learning intention

- I don't know

Grammar learning intention

- Possessive ('s)
- Whose ___ is this? This is ___'s pen.

Grammar rule: possessive ('s)

- We use -'s to show when something belongs to someone, e.g. Caroline's bag (the bag that belongs to Caroline).

Resources

- New language ready to stick in pupils' Remember Books
- Classroom items
- Characters – resource sheet 1a2

Review

Always revise learning from the preceding lesson before introducing new learning. Use the plenary or introduction from the previous lesson in order to recap.

Teaching new language through speaking and listening

Each child should have their own item. Pick up an item of theirs, write and say 'Whose is this ___?' then write and say 'It's ___'s ___'. Show how 'Caroline's' (apostrophe + s) means to belong to someone. Then ask the pupils to do the same with each other's things one at a time (making sure you can hear the apostrophe + s).

Collect all the items (and add four that do not belong to anyone) and give pupils one minute to memorise what is there. Then cover up the items and take one away. Uncover the items and say

'Whose item is missing?' They secretly write down on their whiteboards '___'s pen is missing'. Then count '3, 2, 1. Show me'. Do this three to four times. Then choose an item which does not belong to anyone. Ask whose item is missing? Write 'I don't know'. Shrug your shoulders and say. Pupils repeat.

Continue with the game, identifying which items are and aren't present. If pupils don't know who the object belongs to, they must write 'I don't know'.

Independent learning: write down 'Whose pencil is this? It's Caroline's pencil' (draw Caroline's pencil and show the picture of Caroline on resource sheet 1a1). Pupils complete four sentences with pictures in their Literacy Books. (Wherever possible, pupils should be encouraged to say and/or write the new learning in their home language.)

Extension

'Hers/his' using each other and the characters on resource sheet 1a1.

Plenary

Pick up two more items and ask who they belong to e.g. Caroline's, James's.

Ask the pupils to stick the new language into their Remember Book.

Ensure that you assess each pupil on their achievement of the vocabulary and grammar learning intentions using the assessment for learning form.

Revision

Revise learning from previous lessons by choosing a plenary or introduction from a past lesson that pupils found difficult or focus on learning from the Remember Books.

Lesson 2E

Vocabulary learning intention

- Numbers 1–50
- About
- Friend
- Add (plus) +
- Subtract (take away) −

Grammar learning intention

- None

Resources

- New language ready to stick in pupils' Remember Books
- Number line 1–50
- Numbers 1–100 – resource sheet 2b
- Counters

41

Review

Always revise learning from the preceding lesson before introducing new learning.

Use the plenary or introduction from the previous lesson in order to recap.

Teaching new language through speaking and listening

Show numbers 1–50 and count together. Refer to the written numbers on resource sheet 2b. You say the number, pupils repeat. Then count together. They use counters to count one at a time. Repeat this three times.

Use the counters to show 2 and add 3. Write 2 + 3 = 5. Give the pupils some sums to complete. Then do the same with subtract.

Independent learning: pupils complete the numbers page from lesson 1b in their Literacy Books up to 50. Pupils should continue where they left a space in their books the previous week, with 11 eleven ●●●●●●●●●●, then 12 twelve and so on.

Write down all the names of the people they have met in class. Title them 'friends'. Count how many friends they have made.

Personal Book, title page: This is . . .'s book about me and my friends in . . . e.g. England. Pupils draw themselves at the top and all their friends with the names of their friends underneath. (Wherever possible, pupils should be encouraged to say and/or write the new learning in their home language.)

Extension

Count from 50–100

Plenary

Ask pupils to give you the next number after . . . 43? 21? 33? Then add 4 and take away 2 (according to ability) and so on.

Ask pupils to stick the new language into their Remember Book.

> **Ensure that you assess each pupil on their achievement of the vocabulary and grammar learning intentions using the assessment for learning form.**

Revision

Revise learning from previous lessons by choosing a plenary or introduction from a past lesson that pupils found difficult or focus on learning from the Remember Books.

Vocabulary learning intention

■ School subjects, e.g. Numeracy (Maths), Literacy (English), Geography, History, Physical Education (PE), Religious Education (RE), Information Communication Technology (ICT), Music, Science, Art

■ Verb

■ Pronoun

Grammar learning intention

■ What's this subject?

■ General sentence structure, e.g. subject, verb, object (I drink milk)

■ I like . . ./I don't like . . .

■ Present simple, third person, e.g. I walk/he wal<u>ks</u>

Resources

■ New language ready to stick in pupils' Remember Books

■ Subject labels – resource sheet 3a

■ I like Maths – resource sheet 3b

■ Sentences – resource sheet 3c

■ Pronoun cards – resource sheet 3d

■ Hobby pictures – resource sheet 6d

Lesson 3A

Vocabulary learning intention

■ Subjects: Numeracy (Maths), Literacy (English), Religious Education (RE) and so on

Grammar learning intention

■ What subject is it?

■ It's . . .

Resources

■ New language ready to stick in pupils' Remember Books

■ Subject labels – resource sheet 3a

Review

Always revise learning from the preceding lesson before introducing new learning. Use the plenary or introduction from the previous lesson in order to recap.

Teaching new language through speaking and listening

Introduce the subjects by showing the labels from resource sheet 3a one at a time. Say, pupils repeat. Point to the labels randomly and see if pupils can remember them. Play matching pairs (only use the pictures of subjects and not the labels). Copy two sets of the cards and cut them into equal-sized squares. Turn all the cards over so you can't see them. Pupils play the game as a class but work in pairs. Example: first pair turns over a card and person A says 'What subject is it?' and person B says 'It's Maths.' They then turn over another card and person B says 'What subject is it?' and person A says 'It's Geography.' If they choose two of the same subject cards they get to keep them and have another go. If not, it's the next pair's turn. The winning pair is the one with the most number of subject cards.

Independent learning: pupils stick the subjects from resource sheet 3a in their Literacy Books. Write down 'What subject is it? It's . . .'.

Extension

Try variations of 'what' questions e.g. What colour is it?
What number is it?
What letter is it?

Plenary

Cut resource sheet 3a into pictures and labels. See if pupils can match the subjects to the pictures.

Ask the pupils to stick the new language into their Remember Book.

Ensure that you assess each pupil on their achievement of the vocabulary and grammar learning intentions using the assessment for learning form.

Revision

Revise learning from previous lessons by choosing a plenary or introduction from a past lesson that pupils found difficult or focus on learning from the Remember Books.

Lesson 3B

Vocabulary learning intention

■ Subjects: Numeracy (Maths), Literacy (English), Religious Education (RE) and so on

Grammar learning intention

■ None

Resources

- New language ready to stick in pupils' Remember Books
- Subject labels – resource sheet 3a

Review

Always revise learning from the preceding lesson before introducing new learning. Use the plenary or introduction from the previous lesson in order to recap.

Teaching new language through speaking and listening

Share resource sheet 3a. Ask the pupils if they can name the subjects.

Personal Book, pages 4 and 5: pupils write 'The subjects I learn at school' and pupils cut and stick them into their book. They then label the pictures and colour them. (Wherever possible, pupils should be encouraged to say and/or write the new learning in their home language.)

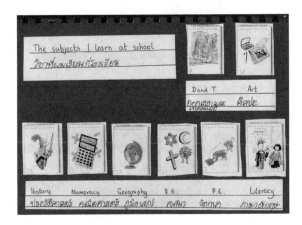 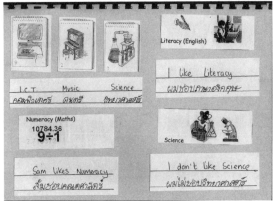

Extension

Share the vocabulary: playtime, breaktime, home time.

Plenary

Point to a subject and the pupils raise their hands to tell you the name of that subject.

Ask the pupils to stick the new language into their Remember Book.

Ensure that you assess each pupil on their achievement of the vocabulary and grammar learning intentions using the assessment for learning form.

Revision

Revise learning from previous lessons by choosing a plenary or introduction from a past lesson that pupils found difficult or focus on learning from the Remember Books.

Lesson 3C

Vocabulary learning intention

■ School subjects

Grammar learning intention

■ What subject do you like?
■ I like . . .
■ I don't like . . .
■ I hate . . .
■ I love . . .
■ . . . is OK.

Resources

■ New language ready to stick in pupils' Remember Books
■ I like Maths – resource sheet 3b
■ Subject labels – resource sheet 3a
■ Hobby pictures – resource sheet 6d

Review

Always revise learning from the preceding lesson before introducing new learning. Use the plenary or introduction from the previous lesson in order to recap.

Teaching new language through speaking and listening

Show resource sheet 3b. Show how pupils might love Maths but hate Science. Introduce the question 'Do you like Maths?' Pupils ask each other what subjects they like. Once they have found out, you ask 'What subject does he/she (the other pupils) like?' Write this on the board: 'What subject does Tom like? He likes . . .' Then invite the pupils to ask each other what subjects their friends like.

Independent learning: choose one subject the pupils don't like, one they like and one they love. Write out the sentences. Then write out one subject their friend likes.

Personal Book, page 6: pupils write 'I like . . .' and stick a label next to it. Then write 'I don't like . . .' and stick a label next to it. Then write '(name) likes (subject)' and stick a label next to it. (Wherever possible, pupils should be encouraged to say and/or write the new learning in their home language.)

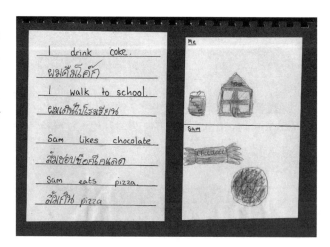

Extension

Use the following words to extend their vocabulary – '. . . is great' and '. . . is terrible'.

Plenary

Show hobby pictures using resource sheet 6d and pick some hobbies such as playing football (which would demonstrate liking PE), writing (which would demonstrate liking Literacy) and so on. Ask questions using the pictures, e.g. 'Does she like Literacy?'

Ask the pupils to stick the new language into their Remember Books.

Ensure that you assess each pupil on their achievement of the vocabulary and grammar learning intentions using the assessment for learning form.

Revision

Revise learning from previous lessons by choosing a plenary or introduction from a past lesson that pupils found difficult or focus on learning from the Remember Books.

Lesson 3D

Vocabulary learning intention

- Subject
- Verb
- Object

Grammar learning intention

- Subject + verb + object

Grammar rule: word order

- We can use subject + verb + object to make simple sentences, e.g. Caroline + reads + a book, I + like + cheese.

Resources

- New language ready to stick in pupils' Remember Books
- Sentences – resource sheet 3c

Review

Always revise learning from the preceding lesson before introducing new learning. Use the plenary or introduction from the previous lesson in order to recap.

47

Teaching new language through speaking and listening

Show the subject + verb + object. Use the example: I + like/drink + water. The pupils think of some more subjects, e.g. I, you, we, a place name, a person, an animal. Then they think of ten verbs, e.g. like, go, eat, drink. The pupils then try and make some sentences with the words collected adding an object, e.g. I like oranges. He swims to France (refer to resource sheet 3c for support). Model this first (you may have to touch on the grammar learning intention for lesson 3e to clarify why 's' appears after the verb when referring to he/she/it).

Independent learning: pupils write down six sentences they have collected in their Literacy Books.

Personal Book, page 6: pupils write two sentences about themselves in their book and draw a picture for each. (Wherever possible, pupils should be encouraged to say and/or write the new learning in their home language.)

Extension

Use more verbs to make further sentences.

Plenary

Use some cut up words (subjects, verbs, objects) to make some sentences using this rule.

Ask the pupils to stick the new language into their Remember Books.

Ensure that you assess each pupil on their achievement of the vocabulary and grammar learning intentions using the assessment for learning form.

Revision

Revise learning from previous lessons by choosing a plenary or introduction from a past lesson that pupils found difficult or focus on learning from the Remember Books.

Lesson 3E

Vocabulary learning intention

- Pronoun
- Verb, e.g. walk, sleep, talk, sit, stand, listen, watch, play

Grammar learning intention

- Present simple, third person, e.g.
  I walk
  You walk
  She walks
  He walks
  It walks

Caroline walks
They walk
We walk

Grammar rule: present simple, third person

- Verbs end in 's' or 'es' after he, she, it or a name, e.g. she walks, he walks, it walks, Caroline walks or she watches, he watches, it watches, Caroline watches.
- For most verbs that end in 'o', 'es' is added, e.g. does, goes.

Resources

- New language ready to stick in pupils' Remember Books
- Pronoun cards – resource sheet 3d

Review

Always revise learning from the preceding lesson before introducing new learning. Use the plenary or introduction from the previous lesson in order to recap.

Teaching new language through speaking and listening

Share three sentences about yourself (note that they should have no 's' at the end of the verb, e.g. I like English). Pupils find out three sentences about their friend, e.g. He likes chocolate. Write the sentences down and highlight that the verb has an 's'. Pupils think of all the pronouns e.g. I, you, he, she, we, it, they. Put the verb next to each pronoun ensuring there is an 's' at the end of the verbs that go with he, she, it or a name e.g. I drink, you drink, he drinks, she drinks, it drinks, they drink, Caroline drinks. Underline 'she, he, it and a name.' Elicit two sentences about your friend and make sure you add the 's' to the verb.

Personal Book, page 6: pupils write down two sentences about their friend, e.g. Caroline walks to school. Then they draw a picture. (Wherever possible, pupils should be encouraged to say and/or write the new learning in their home language.)

Extension

Apply the rule by using different verbs.

Plenary

Cut up the pronoun cards – resource sheet 3d. Ask the pupils to sit in a circle and take turns in turning over the pronoun cards. As each child turns a card, they must make a statement, e.g. He sleeps, I sleep.

Ask the pupils to stick the new language into their Remember Books.

Ensure that you assess each pupil on their achievement of the vocabulary and grammar learning intentions using the assessment for learning form.

Revision

Revise learning from previous lessons by choosing a plenary or introduction from a past lesson that pupils found difficult or focus on learning from the Remember Books.

49

My favourite animal is a cat

Vocabulary learning intention

- Animals, e.g. dog, cat, rabbit, mouse, camel, horse, bird, fish, spider, elephant, lion, tiger, crocodile, monkey, snake, giraffe, frog
- Imperatives/classroom instructions, e.g. turn light off, close door, mind the, be careful, stand up
- My favourite . . .

Grammar learning intention

- a/an
- Plurals s/es/ies/ves
- This, that, those, these
- What are these/those?

Resources

- New language ready to stick in pupils' Remember Books
- Animals book
- Animal matching – resource sheet 4a
- Animal word search – resource sheet 4b
- Pictures of collections of animals
- Plural rules
- Picture dictionary
- At the zoo – resource sheet 4c
- Zoo animal cages drawn on tracing paper
- Imperatives game – resource sheet 4d

Texts

Animals (Penguin Reader)
Publisher: Longman
ISBN: 058278896

1000+ Pictures for Teachers to Copy
Publisher: Longman
ISBN: 0175568782

(If you are unable to find a suitable book then miss the reading activity. The activities following the reading do not rely on these texts.)

Lesson 4A

Vocabulary learning intention

- Animals
- My favourite . . .

Grammar learning intention

- a/an

Grammar rule: a/an

- We use 'an' before singular (i.e. not plural) nouns that start with a vowel sound (a, e, i, o, u), e.g. an elephant.
- We use 'a' before singular nouns that do not start with a vowel sound, e.g. a banana.

Resources

- New language ready to stick in pupils' Remember Books
- Animal matching – resource sheet 4a
- Animal word search – resource sheet 4b
- *Animals* book

Review

Always revise learning from the preceding lesson before introducing new learning. Use the plenary or introduction from the previous lesson in order to recap.

Teaching new language through speaking and listening

Reading: *Animals* book.

Show pictures of animals from resource sheet 4a. Introduce the names of the animals. Say, pupils repeat. Match the animals together.

Write the vocabulary on the board 'What is it? It's a . . .'. Play matching pairs with cut up cards. Copy two sets of the cards and cut them into equal-sized squares. Turn all the cards over so pupils can't see them. Pupils play the game as a class but work in pairs. Example: first pair turns over a card and person A says 'What is it?' and person B says 'It's a dog'. They then turn over another card and person B says 'What is it?' and person A says 'It's a cat'. If they choose two of the same animal cards, they get to keep them and have another go. If not, it's the next pair's turn. The winning pair is the one with the most number of animal cards.

Write, 'My favourite animal is a . . .'. Ask pupils to choose their favourite.

Independent learning: pupils stick the animals into their Literacy Books and write 'This is a ___' next to each of them. The first sentence must say 'My favourite animal is a/an ___' with a picture stuck next to it. (Wherever possible, pupils should be encouraged to say and/or write the new learning in their home language.)

Extension

Complete animal word search on resource sheet 4b.

Plenary

Share the answers in the animal word search on resource sheet 4b.

Ask the pupils to stick the new language into their Remember Book.

Ensure that you assess each pupil on their achievement of the vocabulary and grammar learning intentions using the assessment for learning form.

Revision

Revise learning from previous lessons by choosing a plenary or introduction from a past lesson that pupils found difficult or focus on learning from the Remember Books.

Lesson 4B

Vocabulary learning intention

- Animals

Grammar learning intention

- Plurals s/es/ies/ves

Grammar rule: plurals s/es/ies/ves

- Plural means more than one. When we talk about more than one noun, we usually add an 's', e.g. chairs.
- When we use nouns ending in 'ch', 'sh', 's', 'x' and 'es' we add 'es', e.g. buses, foxes, watches.
- When we use nouns ending in 'y', e.g. family, we take away the 'y' and add 'ies', e.g. families.
- When we use nouns ending in 'f' or 'fe', e.g. wolf, we take away the 'f' or 'fe' and add 'ves', e.g. wolves.

- Sometimes the word changes or stays the same when we talk about the plural, e.g. children, people, fish, sheep.

Resources

- New language ready to stick in pupils' Remember Books
- Pictures of collections of animals
- Plural rules
- Animal word search – resource sheet 4b
- Picture dictionary

Review

Always revise learning from the preceding lesson before introducing new learning. Use the plenary or introduction from the previous lesson in order to recap.

Teaching new language through speaking and listening

Write and draw on the board: 1 bear, 2 bears. Show that more than two needs an 's' at the end. Show the singular (one of) animal and say the name, then show more than one and add 's' to make them plural. Show the rule that for nouns ending in 'ch', 'sh', 's', 'x' and 'es' we add 'es', e.g. buses, foxes, watches.

Look at the other rules for plurals in the same way:

'ies' for words ending in 'y'
'ves' for words ending in 'f/fe'
Plural words, e.g. women, feet, teeth

Independent learning: pupils write and draw an example from each rule. (Wherever possible, pupils should be encouraged to say and/or write the new learning in their home language.)

Look at the word search on resource sheet 4b from the previous lesson. Work out how to make the animals plural. Pupils write the animals in plural form.

Extension

Pupils make their own word search using the animals in the plural.

Plenary

Ask the pupils to give you the name of any noun. Invite an individual child to make it plural, e.g. pen = pens.

Give the pupils a noun with a different ending that requires a different plural spelling for them to find.

Ask the pupils to stick the new language into their Remember Book.

Revision

Revise learning from previous lessons by choosing a plenary or introduction from a past lesson that pupils found difficult or focus on learning from the Remember Books.

Lesson 4C

Vocabulary learning intention

- Animals

Grammar learning intention

- This, that, these, those
- What are these/those?

Grammar rule: this, that, these, those

- We use 'this' for a singular noun that is near, e.g. 'You can have this apple' (said as you give the apple to the person).
- We use 'that' for a singular noun that is further away, e.g. 'You can have that book'

53

(said as you point to a book on the shelf on the other side of the room).

■ We use 'these' to talk about plural nouns that are near, e.g. 'You can have these keys' (said as you give the keys to the person).

■ We use 'those' to talk about plural nouns that are further away, e.g. 'You can have those books' (said as you point to the bookshelf on the other side of the room).

Resources

■ New language ready to stick in pupils' Remember Books

■ At the zoo – resource sheet 4c

Review

■ Always revise learning from the preceding lesson before introducing new learning. Use the plenary or introduction from the previous lesson in order to recap.

Teaching new language through speaking and listening

Cut out two animal pictures from resource sheet 4c (one consisting of more than one animal and another consisting of one animal). Put one picture near you and one far away from you. Point to one animal alone near you and say 'What is this?' Pupils answer 'This is a giraffe' (write on the board and they repeat). Then point to two or more animals near you and say 'What are these?' (write on the board and they repeat). Then write on the board 'They are elephants'. Do this with other groups of animals. Ask the pupils to do this themselves. In pairs, one child says to the other 'What are these?' or 'What is that?' and the other child answers.

Then point to one animal on the other side of the room and say 'What is that?' And pupils answer 'It's a dog'. Then point to a group of animals the other side of the room and say 'What are those?' (write on the board and pupils repeat). Then write down for them to see 'Those are . . .'. Ask the pupils to do this themselves.

Independent learning: pupils stick copies of the animal pictures in their Literacy Books and write the sentence underneath, e.g. What is that? It's a dog (and stick a picture of a dog). What are these? They are dogs (stick pictures of dogs). (Wherever possible, pupils should be encouraged to say and/or write the new learning in their home language.)

Extension

Pupils work in pairs and use groups and give examples of the difference between 'this, that, these, those' for each other.

Plenary

Pupils who completed the extension explain to the rest of the class the difference between 'this, that, these, those'.

Ask the pupils to stick the new language into their Remember Book.

Ensure that you assess each pupil on their achievement of the vocabulary and grammar learning intentions using the assessment for learning form.

Revision

Revise learning from previous lessons by choosing a plenary or introduction from a past lesson that pupils found difficult or focus on learning from the Remember Books.

Lesson 4D

Vocabulary learning intention

- Animals
- Don't, mind the, no . . . allowed, be . . .

Grammar learning intention

- Imperatives, e.g. mind the step, be careful, stand up, don't feed the, don't walk on the, don't take photos, be quiet, don't move quickly, don't eat, no drinks allowed, etc.

Grammar rule: imperatives

- We use an imperative in warnings (e.g. watch out), instructions (e.g. switch on the light), requests (e.g. leave the room), offers (e.g. try this), advice (e.g. don't go to school) and invitations (e.g. come to the party).
- Add 'please' to imperatives to make them more polite.

Resources

- New language ready to stick in pupils' Remember Books
- At the zoo – resource sheet 4c
- Cages drawn on tracing paper.

Review

Always revise learning from the preceding lesson before introducing new learning. Use the plenary or introduction from the previous lesson in order to recap.

Teaching new language through speaking and listening

Write on the board: mind the step, be careful, stand up, don't feed the, don't walk on the, don't take photos, be quiet, don't move quickly, don't eat, no drinks allowed. Ask the pupils to act each verb giving them support for ones they don't know by acting them too. Now show the statements from resource sheet 4c – At the zoo.

Independent learning: pupils write imperatives about their favourite animal, e.g. Be careful of the . . . Then ask them to write two imperatives for their animal, e.g. Don't feed the . . . Then copy the two imperatives about their friend's animal. Draw signs to go with these. (Wherever possible, pupils should be encouraged to say and/or write the new learning in their home language.)

Extension

Pupils work in pairs to adapt imperative vocabulary, e.g. don't talk, don't sit on the.

Plenary

Pupils give adaptations of the imperative vocabulary, e.g. don't talk, don't sit on the.

Ask the pupils to stick the new language into their Remember Book.

Ensure that you assess each pupil on their achievement of the vocabulary and grammar learning intentions using the assessment for learning form.

Revision

Revise learning from previous lessons by choosing a plenary or introduction from a past lesson that pupils found difficult or focus on learning from the Remember Books.

Lesson 4E

Vocabulary learning intention

- Classroom
- Turn off the light
- Turn on the light
- Close the door
- Stand up
- Sit down

Grammar learning intention

- Imperatives, e.g. turn light off, close door, stand up, add, take, point to

Resources

- New language ready to stick in pupils' Remember Books
- Imperatives game – resource sheet 4d

Review

Always revise learning from the preceding lesson before introducing new learning. Use the plenary or introduction from the previous lesson in order to recap.

Teaching new language through speaking and listening

Demonstrate an imperative. Pupils tell you what it is, e.g. Turn off the light. Repeat this again and again. Write them on the board as the pupils guess them. Use the following imperatives: listen (hand to ear), stand, sit, quiet (finger to lips), stand in a circle, stand in a line, say hello, read (pretend to read a book), write (pretend to write), find (pretend to look for something), point to the door, point to the window. Write them down as you say them, then the pupils repeat the words. Ask each child to say one and one of the other pupils carries out the imperative.

Independent learning: play the imperatives game on resource sheet 4d. (Wherever possible, pupils should be encouraged to say and/or write the new learning in their home language.)

Extension

Pupils write the imperatives in their Literacy Books and draw a symbol to show what it means, e.g. an ear for listen.

Plenary

Say different imperatives and get all the pupils to do this, e.g. stand up, jump.

Ask the pupils to stick the new language into their Remember Book.

Ensure that you assess each pupil on their achievement of the vocabulary and grammar learning intentions using the assessment for learning form.

Have you got any brothers and sisters?

Vocabulary learning intention

- Family, e.g. mum, dad, grandad, grandma, brother, sister, baby, pet, cousin, aunt, uncle
- Description, e.g. blonde, black hair, brown hair, long hair, short hair, curly hair, straight hair, wavy hair, bald, blue eyes, brown eyes, black eyes, moustache, beard

Grammar learning intention

- Have you got . . .?/Has she got . . .?
- I have got/I haven't got (I've got)
- He has got/She hasn't got (He's got)
- Who is this?
- This is . . . She's my friend (She's . . .)
- Possessive adjectives (your, my, hers, his), -'s

Resources

- New language ready to stick in pupils' Remember Books
- Families book
- Family picture – resource sheet 5a
- Family picture jigsaw – resource sheet 5b
- Family questionnaire – resource sheet 5c
- Photos of your family
- Photos of the pupils' family
- Descriptions – resource sheet 5d
- Characters – resource sheet 1a

Text

Families (Penguin Reader)
Publisher: Longman
ISBN: 0582448093

(If you are unable to find a suitable book then miss the reading activity. The activities following the reading do not rely on these texts.)

Lesson 5A

Vocabulary learning intention

- Family, e.g. brother, sister, mother (mum), father (dad), grandmother, grandad, baby

Grammar learning intention

- How many brothers and sisters have you got?
- I have got ___ brothers and ___ sisters.

Resources

- New language ready to stick in pupils' Remember Books
- Families book
- Family picture – resource sheet 5a
- Family picture jigsaw – resource sheet 5b cut up before lesson

Review

Always revise learning from the preceding lesson before introducing new learning. Use the plenary or introduction from the previous lesson in order to recap.

Teaching new language through speaking and listening

Reading: *Families* book or share pictures on family picture – resource sheet 5a.

Write and say 'How many brothers and sisters have you got? I have got ___ brothers and ___ sisters' and the short version 'I've got ___ brothers and ___ sisters.' Pupils sit in a circle. The first pupils says 'How many brothers and sisters have you got?' The pupil next to them says 'I've got ___ brothers and ___ sisters.' Go round the circle until everybody has said this.

Independent learning: cut up the jigsaw in resource sheet 5b. Ask each child to make the jigsaw then stick it in their Literacy Books and label the family.

Extension

Pupils use the vocabulary older or younger brother or sister.

Plenary

Look at resource sheet 5a and ask the pupils to point and say what family member they see. (Wherever possible, pupils should be encouraged to say and/or write the new learning in their home language.)

Ask the pupils to stick the new language into their Remember Book.

Ensure that you assess each pupil on their achievement of the vocabulary and grammar learning intentions using the assessment for learning form.

Revision

Revise learning from previous lessons by choosing a plenary or introduction from a past lesson that pupils found difficult or focus on learning from the Remember Books.

Lesson 5B

Vocabulary learning intention

- Aunt, uncle, cousin, niece, nephew, husband, wife, son, daughter

Grammar learning intention

- How many brothers and sisters have you got?
- I have got ___ brothers and ___ sisters.

Resources

- New language ready to stick in pupils' Remember Books
- Family picture – resource sheet 5a
- Photos of your family

Review

Always revise learning from the preceding lesson before introducing new learning. Use the plenary or introduction from the previous lesson in order to recap.

Teaching new language through speaking and listening

Ask pupils to think of all the members of the family. Write their suggestions on the board. Give the pupils a family to look at without the labels – resource sheet 5a – (also use resource sheet 1a3 to help you). Pupils imagine that they are 'Caroline Scott' and then, in pairs, they decide the relationship of the other family members to Caroline. Then they choose another character in your family photo and decide the relationships between you and the rest of the family. You will need to elicit the following vocabulary and write it on the board or introduce it as it is needed: aunt, uncle, niece, nephew, husband, wife, son, daughter and cousin.

Independent learning: in their Literacy Books, pupils write:

'How many brothers and sisters have you got? I have got ___ brothers and ___ sisters.' Or 'I've got . . .'

'How many aunts do you have? I have got ___ aunts. How many cousins do you have? I have got ___ cousins.'

Personal Book, page 7: pupils stick the family picture from resource sheet 5a in the middle of the page and then write about their families. 'I have got ___ brothers and ___ sisters. I have got ___ cousins. I have got ___ uncles and ___ aunts.' (Wherever possible, pupils should be encouraged to say and/or write the new learning in their home language.)

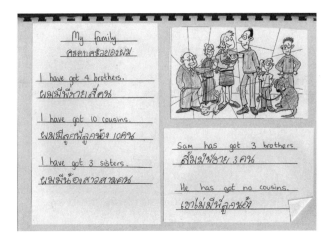

Extension

How many pets have you got?
Objects, e.g. how many pens/pencils have you got?

Plenary

Ask the pupils to bring in some photos of their family for the next lesson. Show some photos of your family again and say who the people are.

Ask the pupils to stick the new language into their Remember Book.

Ensure that you assess each pupil on their achievement of the vocabulary and grammar learning intentions using the assessment for learning form.

Revision

Revise learning from previous lessons by choosing a plenary or introduction from a past lesson that pupils found difficult or focus on learning from the Remember Books.

Lesson 5C

Vocabulary learning intention

- Family

Grammar learning intention

- I have – I've
- She has – She's
- He has – He's
- It has – It's

- They have – They've
- We have – We've
- Caroline has – Caroline's
- You have – You've

Grammar rule: abbreviations

- We often use short forms when we write informally and when we speak, e.g. she has = she's, they have = they've.

Resources

- New language ready to stick in pupils' Remember Books
- Family questionnaire – resource sheet 5c

Review

Always revise learning from the preceding lesson before introducing new learning. Use the plenary or introduction from the previous lesson in order to recap.

Teaching new language through speaking and listening

Write on the board:

I have – I've	They have – They've
She has – She's	We have – We've
He has – He's	Caroline has – Caroline's
It has – It's	You have – You've

Read the long and short forms then read together. Write the sentences on the board to show that both are correct, e.g.

I've got 4 brothers.
I have got 4 brothers.

Ask a child how many brothers and sisters they have got. Then write their answer on the board as 'He/She's got 2 brothers and no sisters'. Ask the pupils to complete the questionnaire on resource sheet 5c and to fill in the sentences at the bottom. Write two of their own.

Independent learning: in their Literacy Books, pupils write three sentences about their friends using the long form and the short form, e.g. He has got 4 brothers and no sisters. He's got 4 brothers and no sisters. She has got 3 aunts. She's got 3 aunts. (Wherever possible, pupils should be encouraged to say and/or write the new learning in their home language.)

Personal Book, page 7: pupils copy the sentences into their Personal Book.

Plenary: one child to share their Personal Book with the class and then pupils ask questions about it or using their photo, ask each child to say one sentence about a friend's family using the short form, e.g. He's got 3 sisters.

Extension

How many pets has she/he got?

Objects, e.g. how many pens/pencils has she/he got?

Plenary

Apply 'how many' to the classroom. Say, 'How many doors has it got?' or 'How many pencils has . . . got?' Pupils can make up their own questions to apply their learning.

Ask the pupils to stick the new language into their Remember Book.

Ensure that you assess each pupil on their achievement of the vocabulary and grammar learning intentions using the assessment for learning form.

Revision

Revise learning from previous lessons by choosing a plenary or introduction from a past lesson that pupils found difficult or focus on learning from the Remember Books.

Lesson 5D

Vocabulary learning intention

- Family

Grammar learning intention

- This is my/her/his . . .
- Who is this?
- Possessive adjectives (your, my, her, his), -'s

Grammar rule: possessive adjectives

- We use possessive adjectives, e.g. your, my, her, his, to say who the noun belongs to. They are placed before the noun, e.g. your pen.

Resources

- New language ready to stick in pupils' Remember Books
- Photos of the pupils' family
- Family picture – resource sheet 5a

Review

Always revise learning from the preceding lesson before introducing new learning. Use the plenary or introduction from the previous lesson in order to recap.

Teaching new language through speaking and listening

Write on the board 'This is my . . .' and show pupils the family picture in resource sheet 5a. Then write 'Who is this?' Using the pupils' own photos, point to each person in the photo and ask each child 'Who is this?' Pupils introduce their families to each other saying 'This is my mother.' 'This is my . . .' Next write on the board 'This is her/his . . .' Pupils swap photos and say 'This is her/his . . .'

Independent learning: give photocopies of pupils' photos to each of the pupils. Each child sticks someone else's family in their Literacy Books and says who they are, e.g. This is his wife and son. (Wherever possible, pupils should be encouraged to say and/or write the new learning in their home language.)

Extension

Use 'their family' and 'our family' in context.

Plenary

Revise the vocabulary using resource sheet 5a again.

Ask the pupils to stick the new language into their Remember Book.

Ensure that you assess each pupil on their achievement of the vocabulary and grammar learning intentions using the assessment for learning form.

Revision

Revise learning from previous lessons by choosing a plenary or introduction from a past lesson that pupils found difficult or focus on learning from the Remember Books.

Lesson 5E

Vocabulary learning intention

- Description
- Hair types
- Eye colour

Grammar learning intention

- Hasn't got (has not got)
- Haven't got (have not got)

Grammar rule: have (got)

- 'Have' is used to talk about relationships, characteristics and possessions as well as similar ideas.
- We use 'have' with I, you, they and we, e.g. I have, you have, they have, we have.
- We use 'has' with she, he, it and a name, e.g. she has, he has, it has, Caroline has.

Resources

- New language ready to stick in pupils' Remember Books

- Magazine with people in it
- Descriptions – resource sheet 5d
- Characters – resource sheet 1a

Review

Always revise learning from the preceding lesson before introducing new learning. Use the plenary or introduction from the previous lesson in order to recap.

Teaching new language through speaking and listening

Write on the board 'I have got . . . hair. She/he has got . . . hair.' Point to someone with black hair (they read and repeat). Show descriptions using resource sheet 5d and draw on the different types of hair. Say 'I've got long, black hair' (use two appropriate adjectives). Arrange pupils into a circle, then go round the circle asking each pupil to use two adjectives to describe their hair. Go round the circle again and ask each pupil to describe the pupil next to them, e.g. 'She has got short, curly hair.'

Next, write on the board 'Have you got blue hair? No, I haven't (have not)/Yes, I have.' Pupils ask each other questions in a circle and answer 'Yes, I have/No, I haven't.'

Independent learning: pupils complete resource sheet 5d themselves and then write in their Literacy Books 'Has . . . got purple hair? No, she hasn't (has not). Has . . . got straight hair? Yes, he has.' (Wherever possible, pupils should be encouraged to say and/or write the new learning in their home language.)

Personal Book, page 8: 'This is my . . . (a member of their family). She/he has got . . ., . . . hair. She/he has got . . . eyes.' Draw a picture of the person.

Extension

Extended descriptive vocabulary/hair types, e.g. frizzy, greasy, dry.

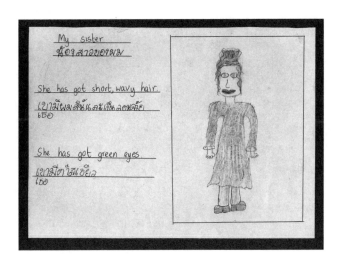

65

Plenary

Pupils describe the characters on resource sheet 1a.

Ask the pupils to stick the new language into their Remember Book.

Ensure that you assess each pupil on their achievement of the vocabulary and grammar learning intentions using the assessment for learning form.

Revision

Revise learning from previous lessons by choosing a plenary or introduction from a past lesson that pupils found difficult or focus on learning from the Remember Books.

I like football

Vocabulary learning intention

- Hobbies, e.g. playing guitar, dancing, drawing, writing, reading, cooking, singing, playing on the computer, watching television, going to the cinema, listening to music, playing games, talking on the telephone, playing sport, playing football
- Sport, e.g. football, basketball, running, swimming, skating, table tennis, volley ball, badminton, tennis, cycling, walking, squash, baseball, gymnastics, hockey
- Ordinal numbers, e.g. first, second, third, fourth, fifth, sixth, seventh, eighth, ninth, tenth

Grammar learning intention

- Can/can't (cannot)
- Likes/dislikes, e.g. Do you like . . .?
- Yes, I do/No, he doesn't (does not), etc.

Resources

- New language ready to stick in pupils' Remember Books
- Pictures of sport that can be labelled (*1000+ Pictures for Teachers to Copy* could be used – see Chapter 5)
- Picture dictionary
- Sports questionnaire – resource sheet 6a
- Sports book
- Sports word search – resource sheet 6b
- Ordinal numbers – resource sheet 6c
- Hobby pictures – resource sheet 6d

Texts

Any sports book

1000+ Pictures for Teachers to Copy
Publisher: Longman
ISBN: 0175568782

(If you are unable to find a suitable book then miss the reading activity. The activities following the reading do not rely on these texts.)

Lesson 6A

Vocabulary learning intention

- Sports, e.g. football, basketball, running, swimming, skating, table tennis, volley ball, badminton, tennis, cycling, walking, squash, baseball, gymnastics

Grammar learning Intention

- None

Resources

- New language ready to stick in pupils' Remember Books

- Sports book
- Picture dictionary
- Sports word search – resource sheet 6b

Review

Always revise learning from the preceding lesson before introducing new learning. Use the plenary or introduction from the previous lesson in order to recap.

Teaching new language through speaking and listening

Reading: Sports book.

Show pupils the picture of a sport – use resource sheet 6b or sports book. Can they guess what it is? Write and say each sport (pupils repeat). Play matching pairs with cut up cards: copy two sets of the cards and cut them into equal-sized squares. Turn all the cards over so pupils can't see them. Pupils play the game as a class but work in pairs. Example: first pair turns over a card and person A says 'What sport is it?' then person B says 'It's badminton'. They then turn over another card and person B asks 'What sport is it?' and person A answers 'It's basketball'. If they choose two of the same sports cards they get to keep them and have another go. If not, it's the next pair's turn. The winning pair is the one with the most number of sports cards.

Independent learning: pupils cut and stick the pictures of sports into their Literacy Books. Pupils label the sports pictures. (Wherever possible, pupils should be encouraged to say and/or write the new learning in their home language.)

Extension

Use a picture dictionary to find names of other sports.

Plenary

Flash different sports pictures at the pupils to see how quickly they can remember and say the sport.

Ask the pupils to stick the new language into their Remember Book.

Ensure that you assess each pupil on their achievement of the vocabulary and grammar learning intentions using the assessment for learning form.

Revision

Revise learning from previous lessons by choosing a plenary or introduction from a past lesson that pupils found difficult or focus on learning from the Remember Books.

Lesson 6B

Vocabulary learning intention

- Sports, e.g. football, basketball, running, swimming, skating, table tennis, volley ball, badminton, tennis, cycling, walking, squash, baseball, gymnastics, hockey

Grammar learning intention

- Do you like . . .?
- Yes, I do/No, I don't

Grammar rule: present simple

- We use the present simple, e.g. 'Do you . . . Yes, I do/No, I don't', to talk about things that happen now, e.g. daily, weekly, sometimes.

- We use 'do' with I, you, they and we, e.g. I do, you do, they do, we do.
- We use 'does' with she, he, it and a name, e.g. she does, he does, it does, Caroline does.

Resources

- New language ready to stick in pupils' Remember Books
- Sports questionnaire – resource sheet 6a

Review

Always revise learning from the preceding lesson before introducing new learning. Use the plenary or introduction from the previous lesson in order to recap.

Teaching new language through speaking and listening

Write on the board 'Do you like . . .? Yes, I do/No, I don't (do not)'. Pupils think of as many sports as they can remember from the previous lesson. Ask the pupils to write down questions, e.g. 'Do you like . . . (a sport)?' on resource sheet 6a. Then model how pupils can use the questions to ask each pupil in the class which sports they like. Ask pupils to ask each other every question on their sports questionnaires.

Independent learning: in their Literacy Books, pupils write three sentences, e.g. 15 pupils like football. 5 pupils like running. (Wherever possible, pupils should be encouraged to say and/or write the new learning in their home language.)

Extension

Do you like . . .? It's OK/A little bit/No, its terrible/I love it.

Plenary

Pupils tell the rest of the class how much they like a chosen sport, e.g. I love football.

Ask the pupils to stick the new language into their Remember Book.

Ensure that you assess each pupil on their achievement of the vocabulary and grammar learning intentions using the assessment for learning form.

Revision

Revise learning from previous lessons by choosing a plenary or introduction from a past lesson that pupils found difficult or focus on learning from the Remember Books.

Lesson 6C

Vocabulary learning intention

■ Sports, e.g. football, basketball, running, swimming, skating, table tennis, volley ball, badminton, tennis, cycling, walking, squash, baseball, gymnastics, hockey

Grammar learning intention

■ Can/can't

Grammar rule: can for ability

■ We use 'can' to talk about ability, e.g. I can swim.
■ We use 'cannot' in the negative form.

■ Cannot is often shortened to 'can't' when we write informally or speak.

Resources

■ New language ready to stick in pupils' Remember Books
■ Sports word search – resource sheet 6b

Review

■ Always revise learning from the preceding lesson before introducing new learning. Use the plenary or introduction from the previous lesson in order to recap.

Teaching new language through speaking and listening

Write on the board:

Can you swim?
Yes, I can.
No, I can't. can't = cannot

Ask each child the question from the board. Ask pupils to think of some more sports and put them on the board, e.g. play badminton, play basketball. Pupils sit in a circle and ask the pupil next to them different 'can you . . .?' questions (they are not allowed to choose the same questions). The next person answers and asks another question to the next pupil. The questioning goes around the circle, one by one, until pupils can't think of any more sports. The winner is the person who doesn't have to miss a go because they can always think of a sport.

Independent learning: in their Literacy Books, pupils write 'Can you play football? Yes, I can. Can Caroline play volleyball? No, she can't.' They write three sentences and choose three sports they like. They stick them in their books and write 'I can . . .' (Wherever possible, pupils should be encouraged to say and/or write the new learning in their home language.)

Extension

Use different verbs to say what pupils can and can't do, e.g. Can you draw? Can you write? Can you speak English?

Plenary

Show a tiny section of a picture of a sport from resource sheet 6b using a piece of card with a hole in it. Pupils have to guess the sport and write it down on whiteboards in context, e.g. I can play . . . or I can't play . . .

Ask the pupils to stick the new language into their Remember Book.

Ensure that you assess each pupil on their achievement of the vocabulary and grammar learning intentions using the assessment for learning form.

Revision

Revise learning from previous lessons by choosing a plenary or introduction from a past lesson that pupils found difficult or focus on learning from the Remember Books.

Lesson 6D

Vocabulary learning intention

- Sports, e.g. football, basketball, running, swimming, skating, table tennis, volley ball, badminton, tennis, cycling, walking, squash, baseball, gymnastics, hockey
- Ordinal numbers, e.g. first, second, third, fourth, fifth, sixth, seventh, eighth, ninth, tenth

Grammar learning intention

- None

Resources

- New language ready to stick in pupils' Remember Books
- Sports word search – resource sheet 6b
- Hobby pictures – resource sheet 6d
- Ordinal numbers – resource sheet 6c

Review

Always revise learning from the preceding lesson before introducing new learning. Use the plenary or introduction from the previous lesson in order to recap.

Teaching new language through speaking and listening

Write on the board the cardinal numbers next to the ordinal numbers, e.g. one, first, two, second and so on up to tenth. Ask the pupils to sit on the floor. 'Who was first? Who was second? Who was third?' Ask them to answer '. . . was third.' Tell them to put their hands on their head. 'Who was first?' And so on.

Independent learning: pupils complete resource sheet 6c. Write who was first, second, third and so on. (Wherever possible, pupils should be encouraged to say and/or write the new learning in their home language.)

Share abbreviation th/rd/st and how it's written, e.g. 3rd, 4th, 5th.

Extension

Write the ordinal numbers up to the thirtieth on the board. Extend the ordinal numbers, e.g. 22nd.

Plenary

Recite together first, second, third, up to tenth. See if the pupils can say up to tenth and beyond without looking.

Ask the pupils to stick the new language into their Remember Book.

Ensure that you assess each pupil on their achievement of the vocabulary and grammar learning intentions using the assessment for learning form.

Revision

Revise learning from previous lessons by choosing a plenary or introduction from a past lesson that pupils found difficult or focus on learning from the Remember Books.

Lesson 6E

Vocabulary learning intention

■ Hobbies, e.g. playing guitar, dancing, drawing, writing, reading, cooking, singing, playing on the computer, watching television, going to the cinema, listening to music, playing games, talking on the telephone, playing sport, playing football

Grammar learning intention

■ None

Resources

■ New language ready to stick in pupils' Remember Books
■ Hobby pictures – resource sheet 6d

Review

Always revise learning from the preceding lesson before introducing new learning. Use the plenary or introduction from the previous lesson in order to recap.

Teaching new language through speaking and listening

Go through the hobbies pictures on resource sheet 6d and see if pupils can match the hobby to the picture. Play a miming game. You give a pupil a hobby and ask the pupil to mime it. The class has to guess what it is.

Personal Book, page 9: pupils write the title 'Hobbies' or 'Sport' and 'I like . . .' (write a sport or hobby) and '. . . (a friend) likes basketball'. They choose a picture to stick with it. (Wherever possible, pupils should be encouraged to say and/or write the new learning in their home language.)

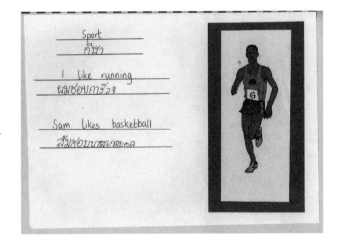

Extension

Pupils use the picture dictionaries to find more hobby vocabulary.

Plenary

Each child tells the rest of the class what hobbies they like.

Ask the pupils to stick the new language into their Remember Book.

Ensure that you assess each pupil on their achievement of the vocabulary and grammar learning intentions using the assessment for learning form.

Revision

Revise learning from previous lessons by choosing a plenary or introduction from a past lesson that pupils found difficult or focus on learning from the Remember Books.

Vocabulary learning intention

- Food, e.g. chicken, beef, sausages, fish, bacon, prawns, hamburger, pizza, crisps, chocolate, fizzy drinks, biscuits, cakes, cucumber, runner beans, salad, courgette, yoghurt, milk, tea, coffee, orange juice, water, cheese, apples, banana, grapes, peach, lemon, chips, potatoes, rice, pasta, bread, onion, egg, tomato

Grammar learning intention

- Countable/uncountable nouns
- Classifiers, e.g. a pack of, a bottle of
- Some/any
- Have you got any/some?
- How much/many have you got?
- I have got . . .

Resources

- New language ready to stick in pupils' Remember Books
- Foods book

- Picture dictionary
- Flip chart page with fridge template
- A–Z food – resource sheet 7a
- Food pictures – resource sheet 7b
- Classifiers – resource sheet 7c
- Food fridge picture – resource sheet 7d
- Glass, packet, can (various classifiers)

Texts

Any basic food book or
Food Alphabet
Publisher: Rigby
ISBN: 0433037288

1000+ Pictures for Teachers to Copy
Publisher: Longman
ISBN: 0175568782

(If you are unable to find a suitable book then miss the reading activity. The activities following the reading do not rely on these texts.)

Lesson 7A

Vocabulary learning intention

■ Food

Grammar learning intention

■ Some/a
■ Countable/uncountable nouns

Grammar rule: countable/ uncountable nouns

■ Countable nouns are the names of things that we can count, e.g. an egg, two tables.
■ Uncountable nouns are the names of things we can't count, e.g. sugar, coffee, sand.
■ Uncountable nouns do not have a plural form, e.g. 'sugars' is not correct.
■ We use uncountable nouns and plurals with 'some', e.g. some sugar, some eggs.
■ We use countable nouns with 'a', 'an' or 'the', e.g. an egg, a packet of sugar.

Grammar rule: some/a

■ We use 'some' to talk about an uncountable noun, e.g. some sugar, some people.
■ We use 'a' or 'an' to talk about one, e.g. a banana, an elephant.

Resources

■ New language ready to stick in pupils' Remember Books
■ Picture dictionary
■ A–Z food – resource sheet 7a
■ Food pictures – resource sheet 7b

Review

Always revise learning from the preceding lesson before introducing new learning. Use the plenary or introduction from the previous lesson in order to recap.

Teaching new language through speaking and listening

In pairs, pupils complete resource sheet 7a (use a picture dictionary when they get stuck). Don't worry if every letter is not found.

Write on the board countable and uncountable (as two titles). Show that countable means you can count it, e.g. 1 egg, 2 eggs. Uncountable means you can't count it, e.g. milk, sugar, rice. You can't have 1 rice (you can have 1 grain of rice or 1 packet of rice, but not 1 rice), similarly with milk (you can't have 1 milk, you can have 1 glass or cup of milk but not 1 milk). Instead, you have some rice and some milk. You also use some if there is more than one, e.g. some eggs.

Ask pupils to label the A–Z of foods with either (u) for uncountable or (c) for countable.

Independent learning: ask pupils to identify the foods on resource sheet 7b. Pupils will already recognise a few, they need to find the rest of them from the picture dictionary. Then ask them to write down five uncountable items and five countable items, e.g. a banana, some rice. (Wherever possible, pupils should be encouraged to say and/or write the new learning in their home language.)

Extension

Extended food vocabulary.

Plenary

Say a food and the pupils tell you if it's countable or uncountable.

Ask the pupils to stick the new language into their Remember Book.

Ensure that you assess each pupil on their achievement of the vocabulary and grammar learning intentions using the assessment for learning form.

Revision

Revise learning from previous lessons by choosing a plenary or introduction from a past lesson that pupils found difficult or focus on learning from the Remember Books.

Lesson 7B

Vocabulary learning intention

■ Food

Grammar learning intention

■ Some/a
■ Countable/uncountable nouns
■ Have you got any . . .?
■ Yes, I have got a/some
■ No, I haven't got any

Grammar rule: Have you got any . . .?

■ We use 'any' when it doesn't matter which, e.g. any food.
■ 'Have' is used to talk about relationships, characteristics and possessions as well as similar ideas, e.g. Have you got any clothes?

Resources

■ New language ready to stick in pupils' Remember Books
■ Food pictures – resource sheet 7b
■ Food fridge picture – resource sheet 7d
■ Picture dictionary
■ Flip chart page with fridge template

Review

Always revise learning from the preceding lesson before introducing new learning. Use the plenary or introduction from the previous lesson in order to recap.

Teaching new language through speaking and listening

Write on the board 'I have got . . .' Ask pupils to say what they have got in their fridge using resource sheet 7d, e.g. 'I have got some milk', 'I have got a potato', 'I have got some eggs'. Use the picture dictionary to help.

Poster: show the pupils a flip chart with an empty fridge drawn in the middle. Ask them to list foods that should be put on the shelves. Arrange pupils in pairs and give them each a shelf for their food. Then write on the board 'Have you got any? Yes, I have got some . . ./No, I haven't got any . . .'. Sit in a circle and the first pupil asks 'Have you got any . . .?' and the next pupil answers 'No, I haven't got any . . .' or 'Yes, I have got a/some . . .'. Write on the board an example taken from the pupils, e.g. Caroline has got some milk. (Make sure they know to write 'has' if they are talking about a name, he, she or it.)

Independent learning: ask the pupils to write six sentences in their Literacy Books, e.g. Caroline has got some milk. Trish hasn't got any tomatoes. (Wherever possible, pupils should be encouraged to say and/or write the new learning in their home language.)

Extension

I/they/we have got some/a . . . in my cupboard/on my table/in my pencil case.
Caroline has got some/a . . . in his/her cupboard/on his/her table.

Plenary

Give each child some food pictures (which they must keep secret) – resource sheet 7b. Each child takes turns to ask another child what food they have, e.g. Have you got any bread? The child being asked must answer in a sentence: 'Yes, I have got some bread' or 'No, I haven't got any bread'.

Ask the pupils to stick the new language into their Remember Book.

> **Ensure that you assess each pupil on their achievement of the vocabulary and grammar learning intentions using the assessment for learning form.**

Revision

Revise learning from previous lessons by choosing a plenary or introduction from a past lesson that pupils found difficult or focus on learning from the Remember Books.

Lesson 7C

Vocabulary learning intention

■ Food

Grammar learning intention

■ Classifiers, e.g. a pack of, a bottle of
■ Yes, I have got a/some
■ No, I haven't got any

Grammar rule: classifying nouns into units

■ We use 'of' with words that refers to units, e.g. piece of paper, packet of crisps.
■ We can make uncountable nouns become countable in this form, e.g. we can count a cup of tea but not tea, we can count packets of sugar, but not sugar.

Grammar rule: a/some/any

■ 'Some' is an amount of something. It is usually used in positive sentences, e.g. I have some peaches.

■ We use 'some' to talk about an uncountable noun, e.g. some sugar, some people.
■ We use 'any' instead of 'some'. We use 'any' to talk about an uncountable noun but usually in the negative, e.g. I don't need any sugar.
■ We use 'a' or 'an' to talk about one, e.g. a banana, an elephant.

Resources

■ New language ready to stick in pupils' Remember Books
■ Classifiers – resource sheet 7c
■ Glass, packet, can (various classifiers)

Review

Always revise learning from the preceding lesson before introducing new learning. Use the plenary or introduction from the previous lesson in order to recap.

Teaching new language through speaking and listening

Show the pupils the objects you have got and see if the pupils know the names of these objects. Write the names on the board as the pupils identify them, e.g. a box of . . ., a can of . . ., a glass of . . . . Give pupils the words to the classifiers they don't know and look at the classifiers on resource sheet 7c. Read the classifiers on the sheet aloud. Get the pupils to repeat after you. Continue to do this until you can point and they can say the name of the classifier without support. Pupils then try to match the pictures to the classifiers on the sheet.

Independent learning: write on the board 'I have got some rice', then write underneath 'I have got a packet of rice' and show that rice is an uncountable noun. Then write, 'I have got some tomatoes'. Show that we use 'some' because 'tomatoes' is plural. The classifier then makes the food countable e.g. 'I have got a tin of tomatoes'. Therefore it does not need 'some' only 'a', unless there is more than one, e.g. 'There are some tins of tomatoes'. Then write six sentences using the following: 'I have got . . .' (2 tins of tomatoes, a can of coke, a packet of rice, 3 boxes of matches, etc.). Pupils must choose the correct way to write the sentence using a/some and not a number, e.g. I have got some tins of tomatoes. (Wherever possible, pupils should be encouraged to say and/or write the new learning in their home language.)

Extension

Extended classification vocabulary, e.g. spoon of . . .

Plenary

One child draws a picture on the board of some food in their classifier. The other pupils guess the food, e.g. some packets of rice.

Ask the pupils to stick the new language into their Remember Book.

Ensure that you assess each pupil on their achievement of the vocabulary and grammar learning intentions using the assessment for learning form.

Revision

Revise learning from previous lessons by choosing a plenary or introduction from a past lesson that pupils found difficult or focus on learning from the Remember Books.

Lesson 7D

Vocabulary learning intention

- Food

Grammar learning intention

- Classifiers, e.g. a pack of, a bottle of
- Yes, I have got a/some
- No, I haven't got any

Resources

- New language ready to stick in pupils' Remember Books

- Food pictures – resource sheet 7b
- Classifiers – resource sheet 7c

Review

Always revise learning from the preceding lesson before introducing new learning. Use the plenary or introduction from the previous lesson in order to recap.

Teaching new language through speaking and listening

Use resource sheets 7b to play matching pairs with cut up cards. Copy two sets of the cards and cut them into equal-sized squares. Turn all the cards over. Pupils play the game as a class but work in pairs. Example: first pair starts and person A says 'Have you got any . . .?' (choose a food) and person B turns the card over and says either 'Yes, I have got a tin of tuna' or 'No, I haven't got any tuna'. If person B has got the tuna, they keep the card and have another go. When they don't guess correctly, it's the next pair's turn. The winning pair is the one with the most number of food cards.

Independent learning: pupils read their Personal Books to each other. They only have one more page left before it's complete. They can discuss who they would like to share their book with, e.g. their class, their parents, their class teacher. (Wherever possible, pupils should be encouraged to say and/or write the new learning in their home language.)

Extension

Pupils use the vocabulary in different contexts, e.g. Have you got any pencils? Have you got some scissors?

Plenary

Share their Personal Books so far with each other. Encourage the pupils to ask questions about the content.

Ask the pupils to stick the new language into their Remember Book.

> **Ensure that you assess each pupil on their achievement of the vocabulary and grammar learning intentions using the assessment for learning form.**

Revision

Revise learning from previous lessons by choosing a plenary or introduction from a past lesson that pupils found difficult or focus on learning from the Remember Books.

Lesson 7E

Vocabulary learning intention

■ Recap on food

Grammar learning intention

■ How much/many have you got?
■ I have got . . .

Grammar rule: much/many

■ 'Much' and 'many' are usually common in questions and negatives, e.g. How many have you got?
■ We use 'much' with singular (uncountable) nouns, e.g. How much sugar have you got?

■ We use 'many' with plurals, e.g. How many eggs have you got?

Resources

■ New language ready to stick in pupils' Remember Books
■ Food fridge picture – resource sheet 7d

Review

Always revise learning from the preceding lesson before introducing new learning. Use the plenary or introduction from the previous lesson in order to recap.

Teaching new language through speaking and listening

Look at the food fridge picture on resource sheet 7d. Ask the pupils to tell you the items in the fridge, e.g. some bread, an apple, some oranges, some sugar. Revise the following rules:

Uncountable nouns = some, e.g. some bread, some sugar.
More than one countable noun, e.g. some oranges, some tomatoes.
One countable noun = a/an, e.g. a banana, an apple.

Write on the board:

How much milk have you got?
How many oranges have you got?

Underline 'much' and 'many' and ask the pupils why they think 'much' is used with 'milk' and 'many' is used with 'oranges'. They should explain that milk is an uncountable noun and that's why we use 'much' and an orange is countable so we use 'many'.

Point to the milk in the fridge and count the cartons together and say, 'I have got three cartons of milk'. Write the answers on the board. Pupils use resource sheet 7d to ask each other similar questions using 'How much . . . have you got?' and 'How many . . . have you got?' and answer using the correct number and the classifier, e.g. 'I have got . . . cans of . . .'

Independent learning: pupils stick the fridge in their Literacy Books and write three questions and answers about the fridge e.g. how much/many . . .? (Wherever possible, pupils should be encouraged to say and/or write the new learning in their home language.)

Extension

How much/many . . . <u>has</u> she/he/Caroline got? (Remember to use 'has' with he, she, it and names.)
How much/many . . . <u>have</u> they got?

Plenary

Tell the pupils you have some food in your cupboard. (Write down a secret item of food.) Ask the pupils to guess what's inside by using 'Have you got any . . .?' When they find an item that you have got, the pupils must find out how much there is by asking, 'How much . . . have you got?' or 'How many . . . have you got?'

Ask the pupils to stick the new language into their Remember Book.

Ensure that you assess each pupil on their achievement of the vocabulary and grammar learning intentions using the assessment for learning form.

Revision

Revise learning from previous lessons by choosing a plenary or introduction from a past lesson that pupils found difficult or focus on learning from the Remember Books.

There is a shower in the bathroom

Vocabulary learning intention

- Home vocabulary, e.g.
  bedroom – bed, pillow, hair dryer, wardrobe, chest of drawers, bedside table, lamp
  living room – sofa, armchair, cushions, coffee table, television, stereo, DVD, satellite, rug, curtains
  hall – stairs, pictures, light, window, door
  dining room – table, chairs, cabinet, photo
  study – desk, computer, bookcase, shelf, drawers, telephone, clock
  bathroom – toilet, bath, shower, basin, toothbrush, toothpaste, soap, taps, toilet roll, towel
  kitchen – sink, washing machine, cooker, cupboards, dustbin, microwave, knife, fork, spoon, pan, plates, cups, blind
  garden – flowers, grass, trees, path, gate

Grammar learning intention

- There is/There are
- There isn't any
- There aren't any
- Are there/Is there . . .?
- Yes, there is/No, there isn't (is not).
- Prepositions, e.g. in, on, under, next to, behind, in front of, near, between

Resources

- New language ready to stick in pupils' Remember Books
- Picture of inside a home – resource sheet 8a
- Picture of a room – resource sheet 8b
- Spider prepositions – resource sheet 8c
- Picture dictionary – inside of rooms (Oxford Photo Dictionary)

Text

First 1000 Words
Publisher: Usborne
ISBN: 074602302

Lesson 8A

Vocabulary learning intention

- Home vocabulary, e.g.
  bedroom – bed, pillow, hair dryer, wardrobe, chest of drawers, bedside table, lamp
  living room – sofa, armchair, cushions, coffee table, television, stereo, DVD, satellite, rug, curtains
  hall – stairs, pictures, light, window, door
  dining room – table, chairs, cabinet, photo
  study – desk, computer, bookcase, shelf, drawers, telephone, clock
  bathroom – toilet, bath, shower, basin, toothbrush, toothpaste, soap, taps, toilet roll, towel
  kitchen – sink, washing machine, cooker, cupboards, dustbin, microwave, knife, fork, spoon, pan, plates, cups, blind
  garden – flowers, grass, trees, path, gate

Grammar learning intention

- There is/There are

Grammar rule: there is

- We use 'there is' to say somewhere, something exists, e.g. There is a car on the road.
- We use 'there is' for a singular noun, e.g. There is a car.
- We use 'there are' for a plural noun, e.g. There are cars.
- We often shorten 'there is' to 'there's'.

Resources

- New language ready to stick in pupils' Remember Books
- Picture of inside a home – resource sheet 8a

Review

Always revise learning from the preceding lesson before introducing new learning. Use the plenary or introduction from the previous lesson in order to recap.

Teaching new language through speaking and listening

Reading: Home page of *First 1000 Words*

Organise pupils into pairs. Give each pair a picture of the inside of the home on resource sheet 8a. Introduce the names of the rooms. Circle all the items they know. Then go through all the vocabulary. Say 'There is a . . .' and write this on the board. Pupils write 'There are some . . .' in their Literacy Books and you write this on the board. Show that 'are some' is only used with plurals by writing two or three example sentences with 'are some' and 'is a', e.g. There are some curtains. There is a bath. Continue through the words saying 'There is a toothbrush' or 'There are some pictures' and the pupils repeat and point to the picture. Go around the picture twice (on the second time, see if pupils can tell you the right sentences with the vocabulary names).

Independent learning: in their Literacy Books, pupils write four sentences with the new vocabulary they have learned and draw a picture of that item next to it. (Wherever possible, pupils should be encouraged to say and/or write the new learning in their home language.)

Extension

Explain that 'is some' is possible if an object can't be counted, e.g. is some sugar, is some tea (not a packet of sugar or a cup of tea).

Write some examples.

Plenary

Give each pair the name of a room and they must write down ten things inside it without referring to pictures or text.

Ask the pupils to stick the new language into their Remember Book.

Ensure that you assess each pupil on their achievement of the vocabulary and grammar learning intentions using the assessment for learning form.

Revision

Revise learning from previous lessons by choosing a plenary or introduction from a past lesson that pupils found difficult or focus on learning from the Remember Books.

Lesson 8B

Vocabulary learning intention

- Home vocabulary

Grammar learning intention

- There isn't any
- There aren't any

Grammar rule: there isn't any, there aren't any

- We use 'There isn't/There aren't' to say somewhere, something doesn't exist, e.g. There isn't any sugar in the cupboard.

- We use 'any' when it doesn't matter which, e.g. any colour.
- We use 'There isn't any' when it doesn't matter which uncountable nouns, e.g. There isn't any sugar.
- The short form for 'there is not' is 'there isn't'.
- We use 'There aren't any' when it doesn't matter which countable plural noun, e.g. There aren't any cars.
- The short form of 'There are not' is 'There aren't'.

Resources

- New language ready to stick in pupils' Remember Books
- Picture of a room – resource sheet 8b

Review

Always revise learning from the preceding lesson before introducing new learning. Use the plenary or introduction from the previous lesson in order to recap.

Teaching new language through speaking and listening

Write on the board 'There aren't any . . . (There are not any . . .)' and 'There isn't any . . . (There is not any . . .)'. Show how the long form becomes short, then show that 'is' is used with singular uncountable nouns and 'are' with plurals by giving some example sentences, e.g. There aren't any pictures. There isn't any sugar. Explain that the noun will always be written in the plural (with an 's' unless uncountable) because we don't know how many of the object we are talking about. Hand out resource sheet 8a and see if the pupils can find the missing items. Pupils must say 'There aren't any . . .' or 'There isn't any . . .'.

Independent learning: pupils stick a room picture in their Literacy Books and write four sentences – two sentences with 'There aren't any . . .' and two sentences with 'There isn't any . . .'. (Wherever possible, pupils should be encouraged to say and/or write the new learning in their home language.)

Extension

Think of lots of countable nouns, e.g. banana.
Think of lots of uncountable nouns, e.g. sugar.

Plenary

Show a child resource sheet 8b. The child must choose a room and say to the rest of the class 'There is a . . . There are some . . . There aren't any . . . There isn't any . . .' and the class guesses what room they are talking about.

Ask the pupils to stick the new language into their Remember Book.

Ensure that you assess each pupil on their achievement of the vocabulary and grammar learning intentions using the assessment for learning form.

Revision

Revise learning from previous lessons by choosing a plenary or introduction from a past lesson that pupils found difficult or focus on learning from the Remember Books.

Lesson 8C

Vocabulary learning intention

■ Home vocabulary

Grammar learning intention

■ Prepositions, e.g. in, on, under, next to, behind, in front of, between

Grammar rule: prepositions of place

■ We use prepositions to describe places, e.g. The spider is <u>under</u> the cupboard.

Resources

■ New language ready to stick in pupils' Remember Books
■ Spider prepositions – resource sheet 8c

Review

Always revise learning from the preceding lesson before introducing new learning. Use the plenary or introduction from the previous lesson in order to recap.

Teaching new language through speaking and listening

Put a chair on the table and put a pen on it. Write on the board 'There is a pen <u>on</u> the chair', then put the pen under it and see if the pupils know the preposition 'under'. Write the sentence 'There is a pen <u>under</u> the chair'. Do the same for 'in' (use a box), 'between' (use another chair), 'behind', 'next to' and 'in front of'.

Show resource sheet 8c. Revise the room vocabulary. Pupils say to each other 'There is a spider in the drawer' and so on. Then, collect sentences on the board.

Independent learning: in their Literacy Books, pupils write four sentences about the spider, e.g. There is a spider on the plate. (Wherever possible, pupils should be encouraged to say and/or write the new learning in their home language.)

Extension

Extended preposition vocabulary, e.g. over, across.

Plenary

Point to a spider and ask a pupil to give you a sentence to go with the spider you are pointing to using resource sheet 8c.

Ask the pupils to stick the new language into their Remember Book.

Ensure that you assess each pupil on their achievement of the vocabulary and grammar learning intentions using the assessment for learning form.

Revision

Revise learning from previous lessons by choosing a plenary or introduction from a past lesson that pupils found difficult or focus on learning from the Remember Books.

Lesson 8D

Vocabulary learning intention

■ Home vocabulary

Grammar learning intention

■ Are there/Is there . . .?
■ Yes, there is/No, there isn't.

Grammar rule: Are there/Is there . . .?

■ We use 'Are there/Is there' to find out if somewhere, something exists, e.g. Is there a bike?
■ We use 'are there' for a plural noun in a question, e.g. Are there any cars?

■ We use 'is there' for a singular noun in a question, e.g. Is there a car?

Resources

■ New language ready to stick in pupils' Remember Books
■ Picture of a room – resource sheet 8b
■ Picture dictionary – inside of rooms (Oxford Photo Dictionary)

Review

Always revise learning from the preceding lesson before introducing new learning. Use the plenary or introduction from the previous lesson in order to recap.

Teaching new language through speaking and listening

Write 'Is there a . . .?' and 'Are there any . . .?' on the board. Give one child a picture of a room from a picture dictionary. The others have to ask questions and decide what room it is, e.g. 'Is there a toilet?' 'Are there any pictures?' The other child answers 'Yes, there is' and 'No, there isn't'.

Independent learning: in their Literacy Books, pupils draw a picture of their living room. They write three questions underneath, e.g. Is there a . . .? Are there any . . .? They then swap books with their friend and answer the questions in the friend's book. (Wherever possible, pupils should be encouraged to say and/or write the new learning in their home language)

Extension

Pupils use a picture dictionary to find more items in the home.

Plenary

Pupils mark if their friend's answers are correct.

Ask the pupils to stick the new language into their Remember Book.

Ensure that you assess each pupil on their achievement of the vocabulary and grammar learning intentions using the assessment for learning form.

Revision

Revise learning from previous lessons by choosing a plenary or introduction from a past lesson that pupils found difficult or focus on learning from the Remember Books.

Lesson 8E

Vocabulary learning intention

- Home vocabulary

Grammar learning intention

- Prepositions
- Are there/Is there . . .?
- Yes, there is/No, there isn't.

Resources

- New language ready to stick in pupils' Remember Books
- Picture dictionary – picture of a bedroom

Review

Always revise learning from the preceding lesson before introducing new learning. Use the plenary or introduction from the previous lesson in order to recap.

Teaching new language through speaking and listening

Arrange pupils in a circle. Go round the circle and ask pupils to say what they have in their bedroom (use a preposition of place), e.g. There is a light <u>on</u> the table.

Personal Book, last page: there is one further reference to this book that allows pupils time to finish. They should consider how to present it, e.g. to the class, to their family. They draw a picture of their bedroom and write sentences to go with it, e.g. There is a light on the table. (Wherever possible, pupils should be encouraged to say and/or write the new learning in their home language)

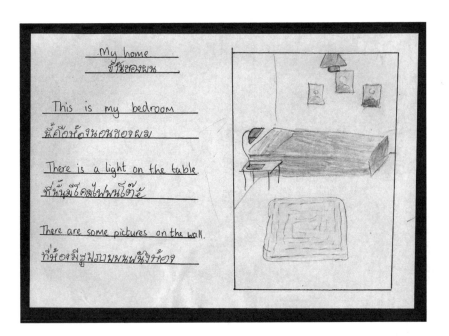

Extension

Write about the classroom using prepositions of place.

Plenary

Pupils describe the classroom to the rest of the pupils using prepositions of place.

Ask the pupils to stick the new language into their Remember Book.

Ensure that you assess each pupil on their achievement of the vocabulary and grammar learning intentions using the assessment for learning form.

Revision

Revise learning from previous lessons by choosing a plenary or introduction from a past lesson that pupils found difficult or focus on learning from the Remember Books.

Can I have a glass of water please?

Vocabulary learning intention

- Sorry
- I don't understand
- Please
- Thank you
- Pardon
- Food
- Waiter
- Restaurant
- Excuse me
- Feelings, e.g. thirsty, hungry, hot

Grammar learning intention

- Making a request
- I would like . . .?
- Here you are.
- Anything else?
- Do you have . . .? Yes, I do/No, I don't.
- Can I have . . .? Yes, you can/No, you can't, e.g. Please can I go to the toilet? Please can I borrow your pen? Please can you pass me the plate? Please can you help me? Please can I have something to eat? Please can I have something to drink? Please can you take me to my classroom?

- I want . . ., e.g. I want a drink, some food, to take my jumper off, to be quick, a jumper, to play, to get dry, to go to bed

Resources

- New language ready to stick in pupils' Remember Books
- Asking permission cards – resource sheet 9a
- Plastic/real food
- Family picture – resource sheet 5a
- What's wrong? – resource sheet 9b
- What do they want? – resource sheet 9c
- Food pictures – resource sheet 7b
- Table
- Chair

Texts

Elementary Communication Games
Publisher: Pearson
ISBN: 0175556954

Play Games with English
Publisher: Macmillan Education
ISBN: 0435250167

Lesson 9A

Vocabulary learning intention

■ Please
■ Thank you
■ Pardon
■ Food
■ Sorry, I don't understand

Grammar learning intention

■ Can I have . . .? Yes, you can/No, you can't.
■ Please can I go to the toilet?

Grammar rule: 'can' for permission

■ We use 'can' to ask for and give permission, e.g. Can I have a glass of orange juice please?

■ We use 'cannot' (can't) to refuse permission, e.g. You can't have a glass of orange juice.

Resources

■ New language ready to stick in pupils' Remember Books
■ Food pictures – resource sheet 7b
■ Asking permission cards – resource sheet 9a

Review

Always revise learning from the preceding lesson before introducing new learning. Use the plenary or introduction from the previous lesson in order to recap.

Teaching new language through speaking and listening

Copy four sets of the food pictures from resource sheet 7b on to cards and revise the foods. Deal out all the cards. The idea of the game is to collect as many sets of four cards as possible. Write on the board:

> Pupil A: Can I have your . . ., please?
> Pupil B: Yes, you can/No, you can't/Pardon/Sorry, I don't understand.
> Pupil A: Thank you.

Arrange pupils in a circle. Playing in pairs, pupil A says 'Can I have your . . ., please?' If pupil B has got any of what is asked, pupil B must answer 'Yes, you can' and give the cards to pupil A. Then pupil A has another go. They can ask any pupil playing. When a player collects a set of four cards, they have a set and must put them down on the table and continue collecting until a player says 'No, you can't' because they don't have any. They must collect as many sets as they can. They cannot put a set down until they have four.

Pupils think of other things they might ask for, e.g. Can I go to the toilet? Can I borrow your pen? Pupils use resource sheet 9a to match pictures to the correct answers.

Independent learning: pupils stick resource sheet 9a correctly in their Literacy Books. (Wherever possible, pupils should be encouraged to say and/or write the new learning in their home language.)

Extension

Can I have her/his . . . please?
Excuse me.

Plenary

Ask some questions using 'can' for permission, e.g. Can you shut the window please?

Ask the pupils to stick the new language into their Remember Book.

Ensure that you assess each pupil on their achievement of the vocabulary and grammar learning intentions using the assessment for learning form.

Revision

Revise learning from previous lessons by choosing a plenary or introduction from a past lesson that pupils found difficult or focus on learning from the Remember Books.

Lesson 9B

Vocabulary learning intention

- Food
- Pardon

Grammar learning intention

- Do you? No, I don't.
- Does he? Yes, he does.

Grammar rule: Do you/Does he?

- We use 'do' to make questions with verbs, e.g. Do you like football?
- We use 'do' with 'I', 'you', 'they', 'we', e.g. Do you . . .?
- We use 'does' with, 'he', 'she', 'it', a name, e.g. Does Caroline like football?

Resources

- New language ready to stick in pupils' Remember Books
- Food pictures – resource sheet 7b
- Family picture – resource sheet 5a

Review

Always revise learning from the preceding lesson before introducing new learning. Use the plenary or introduction from the previous lesson in order to recap.

Teaching new language through speaking and listening

Write on the board 'Do you like bread? Yes, I do/No, I don't/Pardon.' Say it and pupils repeat. Ask a few pupils the questions and ask them to answer correctly.

Write on the board:

	Do	+ pronoun	+ verb	+ noun?
e.g.	Do	you	like	potatoes?

Show the pupils that we make the noun plural as we are talking about an unknown number/ generalising. However, we do not add an 's' to uncountable nouns, e.g. Do you like sugar?

Ask pupils to interchange the verbs, and nouns. Now write on the board 'I do, you do, he/she does, it does, they do, we do'. Change the pronoun to 'he' and ask the pupils what they think will happen to the 'do' (it changes to 'does', e.g. Does he eat meat?). Ask them to work in pairs to create two 'do' sentences and two 'does' sentences on a piece of scrap paper (you check them before they write them in their Literacy Books).

Independent learning: pupils pick out three questions that they have written. They write them in their Literacy Books and answer them. (If the question is a 'does' question, they should ask their friend and then write the answer down.) (Wherever possible, pupils should be encouraged to say and/or write the new learning in their home language.)

Extension

Use 'Do they?' examples using the family picture on resource sheet 5a, e.g. Do they like cats? Do they have a baby?

Use 'Do we?' examples using the pupils in the class, e.g. Do we learn in a classroom? Do we like English?

Plenary

Pupils pick out some questions for each other and answer them.

Ask the pupils to stick the new language into their Remember Book.

Revision

Revise learning from previous lessons by choosing a plenary or introduction from a past lesson that pupils found difficult or focus on learning from the Remember Books.

Lesson 9C

Vocabulary learning intention

■ Food

Grammar learning intention

■ Do you have . . .? Yes, I do have . . ./No, I don't have . . . (any)

Resources

■ New language ready to stick in pupils' Remember Books
■ Food pictures – resource sheet 7b

Review

Always revise learning from the preceding lesson before introducing new learning. Use the plenary or introduction from the previous lesson in order to recap.

Teaching new language through speaking and listening

Give out all the food pictures. Write on the board 'Do you have . . .?' Then write, 'Yes, I do/No, I don't'. Write a food name on the board. Arrange pupils in a circle or a line. Select a pupil and ask them to say to the pupil next to them 'Do you have any . . .?' (and name the food you have written on the board). If that pupil has that food, they answer 'Yes, I have some . . .' and give them the food. If they don't have that food, they answer 'No, I don't have any . . .'. Move on to the next pupil and repeat. Continue around the cirle/along the line.

Independent learning: in their Literacy Books, pupils write two people's names and five foods they had/didn't have. They then write '___ (child's name) has/hasn't got some/a/any ___', e.g. Sam has got a tomato. (Wherever possible, pupils should be encouraged to say and/or write the new learning in their home language.)

Extension

Arrange pupils in a circle. Ask a pupil to ask the pupil next to them 'Does he/she have . . .?' That child must look at the next child's cards and answer accordingly, e.g. Yes, she has some tomatoes. Continue this way around the circle.

Plenary

Ask the pupils 'Do you have . . .?' questions but use things other than foods, e.g. a bicycle, a Play Station.

Ask the pupils to stick the new language into their Remember Book.

Ensure that you assess each pupil on their achievement of the vocabulary and grammar learning intentions using the assessment for learning form.

Revision

Revise learning from previous lessons by choosing a plenary or introduction from a past lesson that pupils found difficult or focus on learning from the Remember Books.

Lesson 9D

Vocabulary learning intention

- Food
- Waiter
- Restaurant
- Excuse me

Grammar learning intention

- I would like . . . (I'd like)
- Here you are.
- Anything else?

Grammar rule: I would like . . .

- We can use 'would like' to offer something, invite someone or offer to do something, e.g. Would you like a drink?

Resources

- New language ready to stick in pupils' Remember Books
- Food pictures – resource sheet 7b
- Plastic/real food
- Table
- Chair

Review

Always revise learning from the preceding lesson before introducing new learning. Use the plenary or introduction from the previous lesson in order to recap.

Teaching new language through speaking and listening

Write on the board:

At the restaurant
Excuse me.
What would you like?
I would like . . ./I'd like . . .
Here you are, anything else?

Read aloud, then the children read it with you. Choose three pupils to perform a role play. Child 1 and 2 sit at a table ready to order food in a restaurant. Name child 3 the waiter. Child 1 says,

'Excuse me' to child 3. Child 3 should walk to the table and say 'What would you like?' Ask child 1 and 2 to choose something from a table using the food pictures. Then child 3 gives them the item and says 'Here you are, anything else?' Swap the pupils round and repeat.

Independent learning: pupils write their own dialogue in groups of three. (Wherever possible, pupils should be encouraged to say and/or write the new learning in their home language.)

Extension

Introduce: 'Sorry, I didn't hear you' and 'Can you say that again please?'

Plenary

Pupils to perform their plays.

Ask the pupils to stick the new language into their Remember Book.

Ensure that you assess each pupil on their achievement of the vocabulary and grammar learning intentions using the assessment for learning form.

Revision

Revise learning from previous lessons by choosing a plenary or introduction from a past lesson that pupils found difficult or focus on learning from the Remember Books.

Lesson 9E

Vocabulary learning intention

- Feeling, e.g. thirsty, hungry, hot

Grammar learning intention

- I want

Grammar rule: I want

- We use 'want' to say what we feel a need, wish or desire for, e.g. I want a drink.
- Want can be followed by object + infinitive, e.g. You want me to go.

Resources

- New language ready to stick in pupils' Remember Books
- What's wrong? – resource sheet 9b
- What do they want? – resource sheet 9c

Review

Always revise learning from the preceding lesson before introducing new learning. Use the plenary or introduction from the previous lesson in order to recap.

Teaching new language through speaking and listening

Use 'What's wrong?' pictures on resource sheet 9b to identify what is wrong, e.g. He's tired, She's thirsty. Write the vocabulary on the board as pupils guess.

Show the 'What do they want?' pictures on resource sheet 9c, e.g. He wants to go to bed or She wants a drink. Match the pictures into pairs. Pupils then guess what the people want from the pictures. Write on the board the answers as they guess.

Independent learning: pupils use resource sheet 9b to match 'What's wrong?' with resource sheet 9c 'What do they want?' and stick pairs into their Literacy Books. (Wherever possible, pupils should be encouraged to say and/or write the new learning in their home language.)

Extension

Pupils play snap with the cards: mix the cards and split them into two piles face down. Pupils play in pairs. One child puts a card from their pile face up into a new pile and the next child puts their card from their pile face up on top. The pupils continue until the cards match, the first child to say 'snap' wins the cards in the pile.

Plenary

A child stands up and mimes what is wrong (choose a feeling from resource sheet 9b). The others guess what's wrong. The pupils say what they want.

Ask the pupils to stick the new language into their Remember Book.

Ensure that you assess each pupil on their achievement of the vocabulary and grammar learning intentions using the assessment for learning form.

Revision

Revise learning from previous lessons by choosing a plenary or introduction from a past lesson that pupils found difficult or focus on learning from the Remember Books.

Where is the library?

Vocabulary learning intention

■ Shops/places, e.g. cinema, restaurant, newsagents, station, bank, library, supermarket, pharmacy, school, park, shoe shop, café, jewellers, market, clothes shop

■ Directions, e.g. turn left, turn right, straight on

Grammar learning intention

■ Where is/are the . . .?

■ Prepositions, e.g. in, on, under, next to, behind, in front of, near, between

Resources

■ New language ready to stick in pupils' Remember Books

■ Shops book

■ *1000+ Pictures for Teachers to Copy* – 'Places in a town'

■ Pictures of shops – resource sheet 10a

■ Picture of a town (containing pedestrians) with some town vocabulary (*First 1000 Words*)

■ Torrington Town – resource sheet 10b

■ Picture dictionary

Texts

'Places we visit' or any book on the local area (in order to introduce the topic)

Shops
Any basic book on shopping

1000+ Pictures for Teachers to Copy
Publisher: Longman
ISBN: 0175568782

First 1000 Words
Publisher: Usborne
ISBN: 074602302

(If you are unable to find a suitable book then miss out the reading activity. The activities following the reading do not rely on these texts.)

Lesson 10A

Vocabulary learning intention

■ Shops/places

Grammar learning intention

■ None

Resources

■ New language ready to stick in pupils' Remember Books

■ Shops book

■ Pictures of shops – resource sheet 10a

■ Picture dictionary

Review

Always revise learning from the preceding lesson before introducing new learning. Use the plenary or introduction from the previous lesson in order to recap.

Teaching new language through speaking and listening

Reading: Shops book and identify the names of some shops.

Use pictures of shops on resource sheet 10a. Try to match the names with the shops (pupils should do this without teacher support – using clues in the names of the titles of the shops). Then complete resource sheet 10a together – read out shop names on pictures of shops, pupils repeat.

Independent learning: pupils stick the shops in their Literacy Books and label them. (Wherever possible, pupils should be encouraged to say and/or write the new learning in their home language.)

Extension

Use the picture dictionary to find more shops/places vocabulary.

Plenary

Show a shop, pupils say what it is.

Ask the pupils to stick the new language into their Remember Book.

Ensure that you assess each pupil on their achievement of the vocabulary and grammar learning intentions using the assessment for learning form.

Revision

Revise learning from previous lessons by choosing a plenary or introduction from a past lesson that pupils found difficult or focus on learning from the Remember Books.

Lesson 10B

Vocabulary learning intention

■ Shops/places

Grammar learning intention

■ Where is/are the . . .?
■ Recap on prepositions, e.g. next to, behind, in front of, to the left of, to the right of, between, on the corner

Grammar rule: Where is/are . . .?

■ We use 'where' to ask about a place.
■ We use 'where is' to ask about one place, e.g. Where is the swimming pool?

■ We use 'where are' to ask about more than one place, e.g. Where are the shops?

Resources

■ New language ready to stick in pupils' Remember Books
■ Torrington Town – resource sheet 10b

Review

Always revise learning from the preceding lesson before introducing new learning. Use the plenary or introduction from the previous lesson in order to recap.

Teaching new language through speaking and listening

Write on the board 'Where is the . . .?' 'It's . . . (preposition, e.g. next to) the . . . (shop name, e.g. shoe shop)'. Say and pupils repeat. Write the prepositions 'next to, to the right of, to the left of, between the . . . and . . ., in front of, on the corner'. Pupils look at the map of Torrington Town on resource sheet 10b and ask you 'Where is the . . . (shop name)?' You answer using the prepositions on the board. Then change the role. You ask 'Where is the . . .?' and pupils answer. Explain that for two or more you say 'are', e.g. Where are the shops?

Independent learning: pupils stick the map on resource sheet 10b in their Literacy Books. Give the pupils five questions, e.g. Where is the bank? Where is the baker's? Where is the clothes shop? Where are the shops? Pupils copy the questions and answer themselves. (Wherever possible, pupils should be encouraged to say and/or write the new learning in their home language.)

Extension

Apply to things about the classroom, e.g. Where is the pen?

Plenary

Say 'It's between the . . .' Give different prepositions and pupils guess what shop it is.

Ask the pupils to stick the new language into their Remember Book.

Ensure that you assess each pupil on their achievement of the vocabulary and grammar learning intentions using the assessment for learning form.

Revision

Revise learning from previous lessons by choosing a plenary or introduction from a past lesson that pupils found difficult or focus on learning from the Remember Books.

Lesson 10C

Vocabulary learning intention

- Shops/places
- Directions, e.g. turn left, turn right, straight on, stop, It's on the left/right, go straight on

Grammar learning intention

- Where is/are the . . .?

Resources

- New language ready to stick in pupils' Remember Books
- Torrington Town – resource sheet 10b

Review

Always revise learning from the preceding lesson before introducing new learning. Use the plenary or introduction from the previous lesson in order to recap.

Teaching new language through speaking and listening

Write on the board 'turn left, turn right, straight on'. Draw arrows to show what each one means. Ask the pupils to walk on your command 'straight on, stop, turn left, straight on, stop, turn right'. Ask an individual child to do this. Write on the board 'It's on the left, It's on the right' and show what this means (using your hands or a picture). Say it, pupils repeat. Show resource sheet 10b and draw a stick person and say 'this is you'. Then give some directions, e.g. 'Go straight on and turn left, it's on your left.' Pupils have to decide where you are giving directions to. Do this two or three times.

Independent learning: pupils write up the new vocabulary into their Literacy Books. (Wherever possible, pupils should be encouraged to say and/or write the new learning in their home language.)

Extension

First, second, third, fourth right/left

Plenary

Pupils read out directions and the others decide where they are going.

Ask the pupils to stick the new language into their Remember Book.

Ensure that you assess each pupil on their achievement of the vocabulary and grammar learning intentions using the assessment for learning form.

Revision

Revise learning from previous lessons by choosing a plenary or introduction from a past lesson that pupils found difficult or focus on learning from the Remember Books.

Lesson 10D

Vocabulary learning intention

- Shops/places
- Directions, e.g. turn left, turn right, straight on

Grammar learning intention

- Where is/are the . . .?

Resources

- New language ready to stick in pupils' Remember Books
- Torrington Town – resource sheet 10b

Review

Always revise learning from the preceding lesson before introducing new learning. Use the plenary or introduction from the previous lesson in order to recap.

Teaching new language through speaking and listening

Write on the board 'Take the first/second/third right/left'. Draw little arrows to go with each one. Read and pupils repeat. Using resource sheet 10b, ask pupils to name some places and you write them on an enlarged copy of the map. Give pupils some directions. They follow these and tell you where you are. Then ask individuals to give the directions and the rest of the class follow to see where they are going.

Independent learning: give pupils a small version of resource sheet 10b and ask them to stick it in their Literacy Books and write some directions. (Wherever possible, pupils should be encouraged to say and/or write the new learning in their home language.)

Extension

Use the vocabulary 'at the traffic lights', 'at the roundabout', 'at the cross roads', 'on the corner'.

Plenary

Pupils say a place and challenge another pupil to give them directions, e.g. Where is the park? The child must accept the challenge and try to give directions.

Ask the pupils to stick the new language into their Remember Book.

Ensure that you assess each pupil on their achievement of the vocabulary and grammar learning intentions using the assessment for learning form.

Revision

Revise learning from previous lessons by choosing a plenary or introduction from a past lesson that pupils found difficult or focus on learning from the Remember Books.

Lesson 10E

Vocabulary learning intention

- Shops/places
- Directions, e.g. turn left, turn right, straight on

Grammar learning intention

- Where is/are the . . .?

Resources

- New language ready to stick in pupils' Remember Books
- Torrington Town – resource sheet 10b

Review

Always revise learning from the preceding lesson before introducing new learning. Use the plenary or introduction from the previous lesson in order to recap.

Teaching new language through speaking and listening

Refer to Torrington Town on resource sheet 10b for ideas.

Independent learning: show Torrington Town on resource sheet 10b and tell pupils they are standing in front of the station. Give them directions and ask them to work out where they are. They do the same. Give them different starting points. (Wherever possible, pupils should be encouraged to say and/or write the new learning in their home language.)

Extension

Pupils create their own adaptations of the map on resource sheet 10b and give directions.

Plenary

Share their maps/directions.

Ask the pupils to stick the new language into their Remember Book.

Ensure that you assess each pupil on their achievement of the vocabulary and grammar learning intentions using the assessment for learning form.

Revision

Revise learning from previous lessons by choosing a plenary or introduction from a past lesson that pupils found difficult or focus on learning from the Remember Books.

Tips on inclusion

Student profile

Collect information to create a student profile before an EAL learner enters the class. This could include:

- Name and nickname – many cultures use a name different to their formal name
- Date of birth
- Arrival date in the country
- Previous schooling and dates of absences
- Place of birth
- Religion
- If the child lives with both parents as part of a family unit
- Dietary needs
- Mother's and father's name
- Most useful written language for the family
- Names and ages of siblings
- Languages spoken at home by mother, father, siblings and grandparents
- Languages used by family members to child
- If the child can read and/or write in languages other than English
- If the child attends mother tongue lessons.

(Based on Hall, 2001)

This information should be used by class teachers before the learner arrives in class to ensure the child's needs and any special considerations are identified as quickly as possible.

Parental involvement

Parental involvement is invaluable for any new arrival. The child's family may be the only people who truly understand their transition. The parents may have very little understanding of what happens in an English-speaking school or approaches to education and it is your chance to show the value in your approach to learning. Parental involvement will help you to understand more about the child's life as well as build a valuable rapport and level of trust between all parties. It is advisable to meet regularly with a parent in the initial weeks.

Often parents of EAL children don't speak English and in these cases, just a quick meeting with the parent and child at the end of the school day would be enough for the child to show their Remember Book to their parents. This will contain everything they learn on a day-to-day basis. This will foster home learning and offer a chance for you or the parent to raise any concerns.

Creating a buddy system

On arrival, set up a 'buddy' system. It is a good idea to introduce or pair the new arrival with other pupils who speak the same language in order for the children to be able to communicate. (The buddy page in Appendix 8 may help.) Obviously this is not always possible and, over time, it's a good idea to change the buddy to a child who can't speak their language so that they have more opportunities to learn. Children could have two or three buddies that look after them during certain times of the day. Ensure the buddy is enthusiastic and a good, friendly, able model. Ask the buddy or buddies to think about what the new arrival might need and provide them with some advice.

One of the buddies can show the child around school to help familiarise them with their environment. Places such as the toilets, the water supply, where to keep their bags and where they meet their parents at the end of the day can all help them feel more welcome. Pairs can use the buddy resource sheet (enlarged to A3 – see Appendix 8) and complete it together. Even with a language barrier, this is a useful activity to help break the ice and start friendships.

Make sure you review the buddy system regularly to ensure it is effective.

Grouping pupils

Research done by Hallam *et al.* (2004) concluded that teachers should 'consider forming specific groups for the task at hand, so as to suit both those who benefit from mixed ability learning, equally with those who are better suited when learning with their academic peers.' According to Gillies (2004), in the structured groups, students:

- Work with others on the task
- Share ideas and information
- Ask each other to elaborate on their points
- Listen to each other.

It is important to offer appropriate seating arrangements and groupings for EAL children so that they are included in the class. Consider the benefits of sitting them next to particular pupils. For example, some pupils are highly organised and would be eager to support the new arrival in the early days. Another pupil may be keen to read with the new arrival or try explaining a concept in the new arrival's home language (assuming you have other pupils who speak the same language). You may find your new arrival to be a mathematical genius that needs another mathematical genius to help with the mathematics vocabulary. Alternatively,

a child who lacks self-esteem may find the role of talk partner really fulfilling.

Effective scaffolding to secure learning

Effective scaffolding of learning by the teacher is essential in whole-class teaching. Bronwyn Danise (2001) looked at the curriculum cycle for scaffolding to secure learning. She identified a cycle that should be given careful thought when teaching EAL learners:

1 Building the field
2 Modelling
3 Joint construction
4 Independent construction.

TA support

If you are lucky enough to have a teaching assistant (TA) working in your class, they can be an invaluable resource to support the new arrival. Not only can they teach the programme, but they can also work with individuals or in groups supporting EAL learners during whole-class teaching activities. They can offer tremendous support to your EAL 'pupil's motivation, confidence and self esteem' in the classroom (Wilson *et al.*, 2003).

Opportunities for extended writing

Extended or creative writing should be fostered from an early stage in the EAL children's writing. It has many benefits from boosting their confidence to giving them a chance to apply or consolidate their learning to new contexts. It is a good idea to build in regular opportunities for extended writing. You can refer to the 'Possible cross-curricular links' section (pages 8 and 18–21) to identify opportunities for extended writing.

Handwriting

It is important to assess and teach handwriting to the EAL learner. The learner may have:

- Written in roman letters before but in a very different or illegible style
- Never learnt how to form letters correctly
- Been used to writing in an entirely different script
- Never used a pen.

Not all primary schools in the UK have consistent handwriting policies and practices (Institute of Education, 2006). However, handwriting is an important element of the curriculum. 'Children who do not learn to write legibly, fluently and quickly may find it difficult to cope with the demands of both secondary school and university. Poor handwriting skills may be just as much of a handicap in the jobs market as poor reading and numeracy skills.' Of course the EAL learner has a long way to go before they reach this stage, but a good foundation needs to be built early on.

Children learning EAL often don't understand that letters aren't about copying marks on a page. They need to know that there is a direction for writing each letter with a start and finish place. The letters they are writing may look like they can write the alphabet, but without correct letter formations it will become difficult for them to start joining their letters at a later stage. These, among other reasons, are important reasons for EAL children to have access to differentiated handwriting support in class.

Considerations – making the new arrival feel welcome

- It seems like a small detail, but make sure the pupil's name is pronounced correctly!
- Allow the child time to listen and be silent in the mainstream classroom. Often they can be too shy to speak and may need plenty of time to listen before they feel confident enough to speak.
- Using other pupils to support the new arrival with learning can be extremely beneficial to both parties. We remember far more of what we teach than what we are told.
- Allow children to use their first language – a natural and helpful tool for clarifying understanding; for example, translating, presenting, summarising or story telling in first language.
- As far as possible, ensure children are integrated into the mainstream class activity, while being differentiated for at their level.
- Where bilingual assistants can support in class, consider telling stories in two languages.
- Involve the children in routine tasks in order to give them a sense of responsibility and inclusion; for example, handing out the books and equipment.
- Sit the child next to other confident English speakers in order to give them more opportunities to use English.
- Ensure they have as much teacher or peer time as possible to explain the tasks.
- Use writing frames, their Remember Book as well as word and sentence banks to provide scaffolding to support independence and as a model for the language to be learned and practised.
- Label items with visuals; for example, a picture of scissors on the scissors drawer or a picture of rulers on the ruler drawer.
- Provide opportunities for recording learners speaking on tape or video and play it back to boost confidence, practise, consolidate, apply or self-assess their learning.
- Consider a consistent use of concept mapping to aid understanding.

Resources

Major resources

Make use of the major resources available.
These can include:

- Other children in the class
- The teacher or teachers
- Other adults, e.g. TAs, EAL specialists, parents, helpers
- The new arrival's family
- The learner's own basic skills, e.g. their mother tongue, knowledge of the world
- Physical resources, e.g. pictures, dual language books, objects.

Physical resources: classroom resource box

Create a classroom resource box of emergency activities as well as independent activities for times when things haven't gone according to plan and you need some support materials to ensure the EAL learner remains engaged and feels included.

This could contain the following:

EAL classroom resource box contents	Resource detail	My review
Readers at an appropriate level	Examples such as: *Meet the Spookies* Publisher: Macmillan Heinemann ISBN: 0435286242 *The Selfish Giant* Publisher: Longman Penguin Readers ISBN: 058245609	These children's books combine basic grammar learning intentions with a set number of words; for example, 100 words which will be repeated again and again in the one story. One hundred words is the minimum for a story and you can get readers with 200, 300, 400, 500 words and so on. The books are good for upper juniors as they are high interest but still cover the basic beginnings of language. Readers can be obtained from the ELT (English Language Teaching) sections of publishers. Penguin Readers are great for variety and sheer quantity of choice.
Oxford Activity Books for Children	Publisher: Oxford University Press Book 1 – ISBN: 0194218309 (There are six books)	This set of six books is full of great English activities which could be used as homework or for pupils working quietly on their own.

EAL classroom resource box contents	Resource detail	My review
First 100 Words	Publisher: Usborne ISBN: 0746041276	Good sources of new words that could be used with a class buddy.
First 1000 Words	Publisher: Usborne ISBN: 0746023022	
First Experiences	Publisher: Usborne ISBN: 0746052960	A lovely book that explains about a child's first experiences at the doctors, going to school, going shopping and all sorts of day-to-day activities that is ideal for a newcomer to England.
Picture dictionaries	Oxford Photo Dictionary: Practise exercises for classroom use or self study Publisher: Oxford University Press ISBN: 0164313603	A great support for all EAL learners. The photo dictionary is very detailed and probably better for upper juniors but really does cover topics in detail; for example, a picture of a bedroom will show almost everything labelled in detail.
	Picture Dictionary Publisher: Macmillan ISBN: 0333647912	This set of two is great for learning dictionary skills and words. It's better for lower juniors.
	Picture Dictionary Skills Book Publisher: Macmillan ISBN: 0333668650	
Buddy sheet	See resource sheet in Appendix 8	This can be used in the first few days when the new arrival is paired with a 'buddy' who can ask them (if they are proficient in the new arrival's language) about their experiences and write in the answers while the new arrival colours the poster. It's a good bonding exercise. If the buddy cannot speak the language, then they may be able to decode some of the poster together and support each other in filling it in.
Numbers 1–100 written	See resource sheet 2b in Appendix 8	Useful reference for newcomers.
Catalogue of pictures	Argos – or other catalogue	Useful for cut and stick activities/naming and so on.

EAL classroom resource box contents	Resource detail	My review
Useful vocabulary sheet	See resource sheets in Appendix 8 (version 1 or 2 could be used) – these are useful words or phrases. They are not to be learnt all at once, but can be made priority for learning. They can be stuck on a desk or the wall at school and/or at home. They could also be entered in their Remember Book.	Essential newcomer vocabulary. Could be stuck on the desk; for example, Can I go to the toilet please?
Visual labels for classroom	See various resource sheets in Appendix 8, e.g. 3a or 2a	Useful labels for the classroom that can be stuck to the appropriate object by the new arrival.
List of high frequency words (sight words)	*Primary Framework for Literacy and Mathematics Learning* (DfES, 2006b)	A list of the most commonly used words in the English language. Extremely useful.

Other useful resources to aid classroom teaching include story props, story packs, dual language texts, big books, posters, magnetic letters, word games, puppets, objects, published language games, home-made games, simple worksheets and story sequencing cards.

Teacher resource reviews

There are also many resources to support learning new grammar and vocabulary, along with many readers. I can recommend all the books listed below and have included a brief review on each. I have used them all with 7–11-year-old learners and have adapted many of them quite easily.

All the books are at basic/elementary level (apart from the books for your own reference).

Book details	My review
Beginning Composition Through Pictures Publisher: Longman ISBN: 0582555191	A great book that offers lots of opportunity for extending English through picture sequences (little scenarios) including sentence/question structures to go with them.
Composition Through Pictures Publisher: Longman ISBN: 9582521254	Same as above but a little more complex. The pictures are invaluable at all levels.

Book details	My review
The Heinemann ELT English Grammar Publisher: Macmillan Heinemann English Language Teaching ISBN: 0435283677	Great picture explanations of basic grammar learning intentions with some lively activities.
Do and Understand Publisher: Pearson Education ISBN: 0582298962	I love this book! It's good for all levels as it contains 50 picture stories sequenced from beginning to end with a framework on what can be said about each picture.
Grammar One Publisher: Oxford University Press ISBN: 0194313611	Lots of fun games and activities to support basic grammar learning. It's a really good book for cutting and sticking and enlarging sections to describe/guess or quiz pupils on.
Grammar Two Publisher: Oxford University Press ISBN: 019431362X	Same as above, but a more advanced level.
Essential Grammar in Use Publisher: Cambridge University Press ISBN: 05215592798	A book for your own reference: a great book that explains all parts of grammar with easy to understand models and activities to help the teacher or pupil grasp the new learning.
How English Works Publisher: Oxford University Press ISBN: 0194314561	A book for your own reference: a bit wordier than the above book, but just as detailed and an excellent source of information.
Practical English Usage Publisher: Oxford University Press ISBN: 019431197X	A book for your own reference: just about everything you need to know, clearly explained. No picture explanations though. Great book.
1000+ Pictures for Teachers to Copy Publisher: Longman ISBN: 0175568782	Wow wee! This is an amazing book. Full of clear, photocopiable pictures of all types on different topics, story sequences, tense structures, word types, feelings, scenarios and lots more. I think this is a must have for every teacher!
Play Games with English Publisher: Macmillan Education ISBN: 0435250167 (Book 1) ISBN: 0435250175 (Book 2)	A good book for adapting pictures designed for classroom games. It includes fun written activities on a variety of basic grammar learning intentions.
Word Games with English Publisher: Macmillan Education ISBN: 0435283804 (Book 1) ISBN: 0435283812 (Book 2)	Similar to the above but using vocabulary rather than grammar for the activities. I also enjoy using this book.

Book details	My review
Elementary Grammar Games Publisher: Longman ISBN: 058242965X	Lots of good speaking and listening activities. Picture-focused grammar games to support learning.

English language schemes of work

Teachers might also choose to supplement the programme with resources found in other EAL 'beginners to English' schemes of work. There are many schemes available. They usually consist of a pupil book and an activity book which progress from basic to intermediate learners. Below are a couple of reasonable schemes.

Book details	My review
Chatterbox Publisher: Oxford University Press ISBN: 0194728005 (Book 1)	Good for Years 5 and 6. There are six progressive books. They start every chapter with a comic strip reading activity. There are six pupil books and six workbooks to go with them. Books 1–3 are better than 4–6. They get quite hard quickly and I think that by the time newcomers reach book 4 they will probably be able to access most of the curriculum.
Happy Street Publisher: Oxford University Press ISBN: 0194338339 (Book 1)	Good for Years 3 and 4 as children are presented with larger pictures and writing.

EAL guidelines: QCA approach to planning and effectively teaching children EAL

The Qualifications and Curriculum Authority (QCA, 2004b) states the following:

Many new arrivals from overseas have English as an additional language (EAL) needs. They may speak, understand or be literate in more than one language and may have some experience of English but will require support to acquire fluency in English and to access the curriculum.

Factors such as age, previous experience of schooling and curriculum content, knowledge of other languages and levels of literacy in their first or other languages will all impact on the development of pupils' language skills and their ability to apply these skills to their learning across the curriculum.

Some pupils may be new to spoken and written English. Others may have learned English as a foreign language, or not be fluent in English even if they come from education systems where English is the medium of instruction. They may also be unfamiliar with the Roman alphabet. Some new arrivals may have had extensive experience of education while others may have had none. 'Children with little or no education' (www.qca.org.uk/qca_5097. aspx) offers guidance on this.

All pupils, including newly arrived pupils from overseas, have an entitlement to a broad and balanced curriculum. 'Planning for inclusion' (www.qca.org.uk/qca_5093.aspx) gives further guidance on steps schools can take to support the curriculum induction of new arrivals, including pupils who do not speak, read or write English.

New arrivals learning English as an additional language need to access the curriculum as quickly as possible. This can be supported by the use of pupils' first languages with peers and bilingual staff and by the provision of appropriate bilingual books and materials to support the learning. At the same time pupils have to acquire English for both social and academic purposes. Provision of support by EAL staff and ensuring the pupils' engagement in active learning across the curriculum are effective ways of supporting the acquisition of English language skills.

By 'Modifying and adapting the curriculum' teachers can provide guidance on supporting the inclusion of new arrivals with EAL. English learning that takes place in the context of curriculum learning needs careful planning.

By identifying new arrivals' prior knowledge and learning skills and by assessing their level of language development, you can set appropriate learning objectives and adjust teaching styles to facilitate pupils' access to learning.

Planning

When planning, you can support new arrivals' learning of English by:

- considering how to inform the pupil of the learning journey the class has already undertaken, identifying skills the pupil may also have developed
- developing a variety of strategies for differentiating objectives
- being aware of the background experience and language profile of the EAL pupil in order to identify variables that might affect progress
- being aware of and understanding pupils' prior knowledge or level of skills
- having high expectations
- analysing the language and cognitive demands of lesson content at vocabulary, syntax and discourse levels, and having an understanding of how they can be used to promote language as well as content learning
- planning collaborative work with contextual support, including guided and supported group work
- providing ample opportunities for pupils to hear good models of a range of styles and registers of English
- providing opportunities for talk, whilst being aware that pupils with EAL may need time before being able or confident to engage in speaking

- carefully scaffolding reading activities, for example using paired reading and directed activities related to texts
- preparing to teach language skills explicitly, including demonstrating grammar conventions, with opportunities to practise language use
- preparing tasks that are clear, purposeful, practical and that build on prior knowledge. Pupils can be engaged in practical activities with users of English that match the pupils' language-development needs
- planning with specialist or other support staff for their effective deployment. This may involve planning whole-class, small group and individual learning activities, or planning to provide pre-teaching or tutoring. For example, support staff may work with pupils before the lesson to introduce and practise language, discuss concepts, read text to be used in the lesson and clarify meanings
- preparing resources that support the development of pupils' English language skills and understanding, including **visuals** and key visuals or graphic organisers (for example timelines, tree diagrams, flow charts, tables, graphs, pie charts and cycle diagrams) to support understanding of key words and concepts, *a supportive print environment* that is visible and related to the topic of study, including bilingual labels and dictionaries if appropriate, and *culturally relevant resources* to increase motivation and involvement.

Teaching strategies

When teaching, staff can use a range of strategies to support English language acquisition by:

- activating peer support
- supporting pupils' understanding by

continually introducing, explaining and illustrating key vocabulary related to subject content

- scaffolding writing tasks, for example modelling writing action (such as correct letter formation), matching, sequencing, providing writing frames and word banks
- scaffolding oracy, for example using frameworks for talking and active listening tasks
- modelling oral and written language to support acquisition
- using ICT programs to support language skills and to reinforce learning
- regularly monitoring pupils' understanding in ways that do not involve the use of English only
- exploiting previously used language to activate prior knowledge and link to pupils' experience
- integrating speaking, listening, reading and writing in English, and using one language skill to support and reinforce another
- reinforcing language learning and understanding through repetition, highlighting vocabulary learnt, summarising and recording what has been learnt and creating opportunities to revisit key concepts through questioning
- encouraging pupil responses and promoting interaction using different forms of questioning: closed and open, concrete and abstract, and higher-order questions
- using culturally accessible learning materials
- ensuring each pupil experiences success, for example through differentiation including the differentiation of homework tasks
- promoting thinking and talking in first languages to support understanding.

Pupils should be encouraged to use their first language in lessons when:

- the cognitive challenge is likely to be high
- they are still developing proficiency in English
- oral rehearsal will help reflection.

To facilitate pupils using their first language you may:

- have additional support for EAL learners
- be able to use the expertise of the EMA teacher in school or in the LEA to help you plan ways in which pupils learning EAL can reach their maximum levels of attainment
- be able to group EAL learners who share a home language. Such pupils may be able to support each other's understanding through the use of their first language to explore concepts and ideas before moving into the use of English
- use visual clues and resources to help make the meaning clearer
- highlight key words and give them to the pupil in English and in their home language.

As with all learners, pupils learning EAL should be encouraged to become increasingly independent in their learning. If a pupil appears fluent in social English, it is still important to plan carefully for language development so the pupil can manage the literacy demands of curriculum subjects.

The national strategies are intended to provide newly arrived pupils with positive experiences of learning English as an additional language with focused attention on language learning.

Baseline assessment

1. What's your name? _____ (unit 1)

2. How old are you? _____ (unit 1)

3. Where do you come from?_____ (unit 1)

4. Where do you live?_____ (unit 1)

5. a   b   c   d   _   _   _   _   _   _   k   l   m   n

    _   _   _   _   _   _   _   v   w   _   _   _   (unit 1)

6. 1   2   3   _   _   _   _   _   _   _   _   _   _   (unit 1)

7a. Colour the boxes: 7b. Answer the questions.

black   ███████ ⟶   e.g. *Is it black? Yes, it is.*

red   ☐   ⟶   Is it orange? No, _____

orange   ☐   ⟶   Is it yellow?_____

blue   ☐   ⟶   _____ Yes, it is.

yellow   ☐   ⟶   _____ No, it isn't. (unit 1)

8. What is this?

e.g. *It is a pen.*   _____   _____

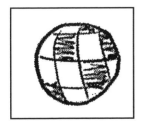  

e.g. *It is a ball* _____ _____

(unit 2)

9. 1 + 2 = _____

4 + 5 = _____

24 + 32 = _____

10. 5 – 1 = _____

9 – 4 = _____

21 – 5 = _____

(unit 2)

11.

Caroline's computer Tom's balloon James's teddy

Whose computer is this? *It's Caroline's computer.*

Whose balloon is this? _____

Whose teddy is this? _____ (unit 2)

12. Underline the answer: *a*, *b* or *c*.

Caroline___ ball

a. Carolines ball
b. Caroline's ball
c. Caroline ball

Tom___ pen

a. Toms pen
b. Tom pen
c. Tom's pen

(unit 2)

13. Complete:

<u>15</u> <u>16</u> <u>17</u> <u>18</u> <u>19</u> <u>20</u> __ __ __ __ __ 26 __ __

__ __ __ __ __ __ __ __ __ __ __

__ __ __ __ __ __ __ __ __ __

(unit 2)

14. What's this in English?   What's this in English?

e.g. *It's a door*.   It's_____

What's this in English?   What's this in English?

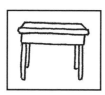   

It's _____   It's _____   (unit 2)

15. Underline *his* or *her*.

e.g. This is *his*/her pen.   This is *his/her* pen.   This is *his/her* computer.

120

This is *his/her* ball.   This is *his/her* balloon.   (unit 2)

16. Think of some more words to go with each picture.

<u>Food</u> (unit 8)   <u>Sports</u> (unit 6)   <u>Subjects</u> (unit 3)

e.g. *apple*   e.g. *table tennis*   e.g. *Art*

_____   _____   _____

_____   _____   _____

_____   _____   _____

<u>Animals</u> (unit 4)   <u>Family</u> (unit 5)

e.g. *dog*   e.g. *mum*

_____   _____

_____   _____

_____   _____

121

17. Write the sentence using the correct verb.

I [image] to school.   I [image] to the teacher.

e.g. *I walk to school.*   _____

I [image] water.   I [image] games.

_____   _____

[image]

_____ (unit 3)

18a. Fill in the gaps.

Do you like Art? _____

Do you like Geography? _____

_____? Yes, I like _____

18b. What subject is it? _____ [image: Hello~!]

_____ (unit 3)

19. Underline the answer: *a*, *b*, *c* or *d*.

She ____ on the chair.

a. is sit   b. sits   c. sit's   d. sit

He ____ home.

a. walk   b. walker   c. walks   d. walking   (unit 4)

20.   Write a sentence (imperative) to go with the picture.

e.g. *Close the door*.   _____

_____   _____ (unit 4)

21.   Label the plural pictures.

e.g. *pens*_____   _____

_____   _____ (unit 4)

22.   What's your favourite animal?

_____ (unit 4)

123

23. What are these?

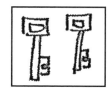
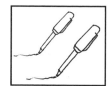

e.g. *These are keys.*   _____ (unit 4)

What are those?

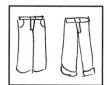

_____   _____ (unit 4)

24a. Describe Grandad.

e.g. *He has got short hair.*

He has got _____

He has got _____

_____

_____

24b.

Has she got short hair?   Has he got a beard?

_____   _____

Have you got blue eyes? _____

Have you got a sister? _____ (unit 5)

124

25. Fill in the gaps.

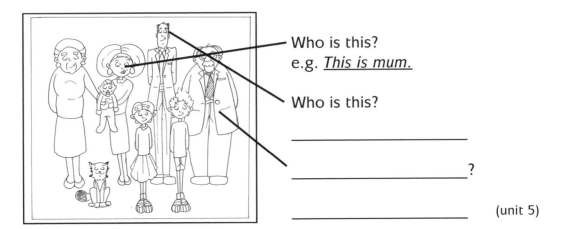

Who is this?
e.g. _This is mum._

Who is this?

_____

_____ ?

_____ (unit 5)

26. Label these hobbies:

e.g. _playing football_

_____ _____ _____

(unit 6)

27. Label.

e.g. _1st_ = _first_

_2nd_ = _____

_3rd_ = _____

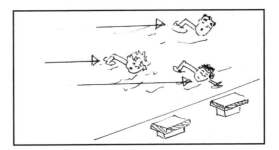

(unit 6)

28. Underline the answer: _a, b, c_ or _d_.

Can he swim?

a. Yes, he can.   b. Yes, he has.

c. Yes, he can't.   d. Yes, it isn't.

125

Can she play guitar?

a. Yes, she can.   b. Yes, she have.

c. No, she can't.   d. Yes, it isn't.

(unit 6)

29. Answer the questions:

Does Caroline like dancing?   Does Edd like playing sport?

_____   _____ (unit 6)

30. Match the following:

tin of ———————— crisps
bag of   beans
packet of   clothes
bottle of   water   (unit 7)

31. Write in: *a* or *some*

e.g. *some* rice   _____ water

_____ bottle of water   _____ bag of rice   (unit 7)

32. Fill in the gaps:

→ chicken

e.g. *Has she got any chicken?*
Yes, she has got some chicken.

→ pizza

Has he got any ice cream?

_____

Has she _____?

Yes, she _____ (unit 7)

33. Underline *much* or *many*.

e.g. How <u>*much*</u>/*many* rice has he got?

How *much*/*many* bananas has she got?

How *much*/*many* milk has she got?

How *much*/*many* oranges has he got?

How *much*/*many* chicken has he got?

(unit 7)

34. Write some more examples:

<u>Home</u> (unit 8)

<u>Shops/places</u> (unit 10)

<u>Clothes</u> (unit 3)

television

hairdressers

trousers

_____

_____

_____

_____

_____

_____

_____

_____

_____

127

35. Underline *are* or *is* and complete the answer.

e.g. <u>*Are*</u>/*is* there any trousers in the wardrobe?
<u>*Yes, there are.*</u>

Are/is there any socks in the wardrobe?

_____ , there _____

Are/is there a shirt in the wardrobe?

_____

(unit 8)

36. Where is the mouse?

e.g. <u>*There is a mouse under the table.*</u>

There is a mouse _____

There is a mouse _____

Is there a mouse under the table?

_____

(unit 8)

37. Fill in the gaps.

e.g. I feel <u>*thirsty*</u>.　　I feel _____　　I feel _____

(unit 9)

38. Fill in the gaps.

Would you like some food?

Would you like a drink?

e.g. <u>*No, I wouldn't like any milk thank you.*</u>

Yes, _____

_____ (unit 9)

128

39. Fill in the gaps.

Do you have any bananas? _____

Do you have any bread? _____

_____? No, I don't.

_____? Yes, I do.   (unit 9)

40. Fill in the gaps.

e.g. *Can I have a glass of water?*   *Yes, you can.*

Can I have _____? No, _____

_____? Yes, you can.   (unit 9)

41. Look at the picture and say what you *want*.

e.g. *I want a glass*   _____   _____
of milk.

_____   _____

(unit 9)

42. Complete the directions.

Where is the library?

Go straight on, _____

_____

_____

_____ (unit 10)

129

Baseline assessment answers

1. What's your name? My name is . . .   (unit 1)

2. How old are you? I am . . .   (unit 1)

3. Where do you come from? I come from . . .   (unit 1)

4. Where do you live? I live in . . .   (unit 1)

5. a b c d e f g h i j k l m n o p q r s t u v w x y z   (unit 1)

6. 1 2 3 4 5 6 7 8 9 10 11 12 13 14   (unit 1)

7a. Colour the boxes in the colour stated.

7b. Is it orange? No, it isn't.
    Is it yellow? No, it isn't.
    Is it blue? Yes, it is.
    Is it orange? No, it isn't.   (unit 1)

8. What is this? It is a book. It is a pencil. It is an elephant. It is an envelope.   (unit 2)

9. $1 + 2 = 3, 4 + 5 = 9, 24 + 32 = 56$

10. $5 - 1 = 4, 9 - 4 = 5, 21 - 5 = 16$ (unit 2)

11. Whose balloon is this? It's Tom's balloon.
    Whose teddy is this? It's James's teddy.   (unit 2)

12. a. Carolines ball   b. Caroline's ball   c. Caroline ball
    a. Toms pen   b. Tom pen   c. Tom's pen   (unit 2)

13. 15 16 17 18 19 20 21 22 23 24 25 26 27 28 29 30 31 32 33 34
    35 36 37 38 39 40 41 42 43 44 45 46 47 48 49 50   (unit 2)

14. What's this in English? It's a chair. It's a table. It's a cat.   (unit 2/3)

15. This is *his/her* pen. This is *his*/her computer. This is *his/her* ball.
    This is *his*/her balloon.   (unit 2)

16. Examples could include: Food: orange, pizza, bread, rice   (unit 8)
    Sports: football, tennis, volley ball, basketball   (unit 6)
    Subjects: Art, Maths, Literacy, Science   (unit 3)
    Animals: cat, horse, donkey, cow   (unit 4)
    Family: sister, brother, aunt, dad   (unit 5)

17. I listen to the teacher. I drink water. I play games. I sleep in my bed. (unit 3)

18a. Yes, I like Art. Or No, I don't like Art. Yes, I like Geography. Or No, I don't like Geography. Example: Do you like Science? Yes, I like Science. (unit 3)

18b. The subject is English or Literacy. (unit 3)

19. a. is sit   a. walk
    <u>b. sits</u>   b. walker
    c. sit's   <u>c. walks</u>
    d. sit   d. walking (unit 4)

20. Switch on the light. Sit down. Come here. (unit 4)

21. birds, buses, children

22. What's your favourite animal? My favourite animal is (children write an animal). (unit 4)

23. What are these? These are pens. What are those? Those are trousers. Those are tables. (unit 4)

24a. Describe Grandad. The child must use 'has got' in context. *He has got* a big nose. He has got a tie. He has got a jacket. He has got a belt. He has got shoes. He has got a moustache.

24b. Has she got short hair? No, she hasn't. Has he got a beard? No, he hasn't. Have you got blue eyes? Yes, I have. Or No, I haven't. Have you got a sister? Yes, I have. Or No, I haven't. (unit 5)

25. Who is this? This is dad. Who is this? This is grandad. (unit 5)

26. cooking, painting, watching television (unit 6)

27. 2nd = second, 3rd = third (unit 6)

28. <u>a. Yes, he can.</u>   a. Yes, she can.
    b. Yes, he has.   b. Yes, she have.
    c. Yes, he can't.   <u>c. No, she can't.</u>
    d. Yes, it isn't.   d. Yes, it isn't. (unit 6)

29. Does Caroline like dancing? Yes, she does. Does Edd like playing sport? No, he doesn't. (unit 6)

30. bag of clothes, packet of crisps, bottle of water (unit 7)

31. a bottle of water, some water, a bag of rice (unit 7)

32. Has he got any ice cream? No, he hasn't. Has she got a drink? Yes, she has. (unit 7)

33. How *much/<u>many</u>* bananas has she got? How <u>*much*</u>/*many* milk has she got? How *much/<u>many</u>* oranges has he got? How <u>*much*</u>/*many* chicken has he got? (unit 7)

131

34. Examples could include:
    Home: television, table, sofa, light (unit 8)
    Shops/places: café, market, park, supermarket, library, school (unit 10)
    Clothes: shoes, ties, shirt, skirt (unit 3)

35. _Are_/is there any socks in the wardrobe? Yes, there are. _Are_/_is_ there a shirt in
    the wardrobe? No, there isn't. (unit 8)

36. Where is the mouse? There is a mouse on the table. There is a mouse beside
    the table. Is there a mouse under the table? Yes, there is a mouse under the table. (unit 8)

37. I feel cold. I feel wet. (unit 9)

38. Would you like some food? Yes, I would like some food please. (unit 9)

39. Do you have any bananas? Yes, I do. Do you have any bread? No, I don't.
    E.g. Do you have any pineapples? No, I don't. E.g. Do you have any tomatoes?
    Yes, I do. (unit 9)

40. E.g. Can I have some chicken? No, you can't. Can I have some sausages?
    Yes, you can. (unit 9)

41. I want a glass of orange juice. I want a jumper. (unit 9)

42. Go straight on, turn right, go straight on, take the first left and it's on your right. (unit 10)

Assessment for learning forms

Assessment for learning of Unit 1: Getting to know you

Pupil name and understanding △ (see p. 14)

The pupil can successfully:	Names:	Notes for future planning
Use 'hello' and 'goodbye' Not formally assessed (From lesson 1a)		
Spell their name Baseline assessment question 1 (From lesson 1a)		
Use 'What's your name? My name is . . .' Baseline assessment question 1 (From lesson 1a)		
Use 'How old are you? I am . . . years old' Baseline assessment question 2 (From lesson 1b)		
Use 'I come from . . .' Baseline assessment question 3 (From lesson 1c)		
Use 'I live in . . .' Baseline assessment question 4 (From lesson 1c)		
Use a full stop Baseline assessment questions 1–4 (From lesson 1d)		
Use capitals at the beginnings of sentences Baseline assessment questions 1–4 (From lesson 1d)		

Say and write the alphabet Baseline assessment question 5 (From lesson 1d)				
Use numbers 1–11 Baseline assessment question 6 (From lesson 1b)				
Use colours in context Baseline assessment question 7a (From lesson 1e)				
Use 'Yes' and 'No' Baseline assessment question 7b (From lesson 1e)				
Use 'Is this blue? Yes, it is/No, it isn't' Baseline assessment question 7b (From lesson 1e)				
Use a question mark at the end of a question Baseline assessment question 7b (From lesson 1d)				

Assessment for learning of Unit 2: What's this in English?   Names:

Pupil name and understanding △ (see p. 14)

Notes for future planning

The pupil can successfully:

Use classroom vocabulary. e.g. pen, pencil, ruler, table
Baseline assessment question 8
(From lesson 2a)

Use 'What's this? What's that? It's a . . ./ It isn't a . . .'
Baseline assessment question 8
(From lesson 2b)

Use a/an + the (vowel + an)
Baseline assessment question 8
(From lesson 2a)

Add
Baseline assessment question 9
(From lesson 2e)

Subtract
Baseline assessment question 10
(From lesson 2e)

Use 'Whose . . . is this? This is . . . pen.'
Baseline assessment question 11
(From lesson 2d)

Use possessive -'s
Baseline assessment question 12
(From lesson 2d)

Use numbers 1–50
Baseline assessment question 13
(From lesson 2e)

Use 'What's this/that in English?' (What is) Baseline assessment question 14 (From lesson 2b)							
Use possessive adjectives, e.g. your, my Baseline assessment question 15 (From lesson 2c)							
Use vowels Not formally assessed (From lesson 2a)							
Use 'I don't know' Not formally assessed (From lesson 2d)							

Assessment for learning of Unit 3: I like Literacy

Pupil name and understanding △ (see p. 14)

Names:

The pupil can successfully:	Notes for future planning
Use basic nouns Baseline assessment question 14 (From lesson 3d)	
Use school subjects Baseline assessment question 16 (From lesson 3a)	
Use basic verbs Baseline assessment question 17 (From lesson 3e)	
Use general sentence structure, e.g. subject, verb, object (I drink milk) Baseline assessment question 17 (From lesson 3d)	
Use 'I like . . ./I don't like . . .' Baseline assessment question 18a (From lesson 3c)	
Use present simple, e.g. I walk/he walks Baseline assessment question 19 (From lesson 3e)	
Use 'What subject is it?' Baseline assessment question 18b (From lesson 3a)	

Assessment for learning of Unit 4: My favourite animal is a cat

Pupil name and understanding △ (see p. 14)

The pupil can successfully:	Names:									Notes for future planning
Use animal names Baseline assessment question 16 (From lesson 4a)										
Use imperatives/classroom instructions. e.g. close the door Baseline assessment question 20 (From lesson 4e)										
Use plurals s/es Baseline assessment question 21 (From lesson 4b)										
Use 'My favourite . . .' Baseline assessment question 22 (From lesson 4a)										
Use 'These, that, those' Baseline assessment question 23 (From lesson 4c)										

139

Assessment for learning of Unit 5: Have you got any brothers and sisters?

Names:

Pupil name and understanding △ (see p. 14)

The pupil can successfully:									Notes for future planning
Use family vocabulary
Baseline assessment question 16
(From lesson 5a)									
Describe a person
Baseline assessment question 24a
(From lesson 5e)									
Use 'I have got/I haven't got (I've got). Have you got . . .?/Has she got . . .?'
Baseline assessment question 24b
(From lesson 5b)									
Use 'Who is this? This is . . . She's my friend (She's . . .)'
Baseline assessment question 25
(From lesson 5d)									
Use possessive adjectives (your, my, her, his), - 's
Baseline assessment question 15
(From lesson 5d)									

Assessment for learning of Unit 6: I like football

Pupil name and understanding △ (see p. 14)

The pupil can successfully:	Names:								Notes for future planning
Use sport vocabulary Baseline assessment question 16 (From lesson 6a)									
Use hobbies vocabulary Baseline assessment question 26 (From lesson 6e)									
Use ordinal numbers (first, second, third) Baseline assessment question 27 (From lesson 6d)									
Use can/can't (cannot) Baseline assessment question 28 (From lesson 6c)									
Use likes/dislikes, e.g. Do you like . . .? Yes, I do/No, he doesn't (does not) Baseline assessment question 29 (From lesson 6b)									

Assessment for learning of Unit 7: Have you got any sugar?

Pupil name and understanding △ (see p. 14)

The pupil can successfully:	Names:									Notes for future planning
Use food vocabulary Baseline assessment question 16 (From lesson 7a)										
Use classifiers of quantity, e.g. a bottle of, a pack of Baseline assessment question 30 (From lesson 7c)										
Use countable/uncountable nouns in context Baseline assessment question 31 (From lesson 7a)										
Use 'Has she got any . . .?' Baseline assessment question 32 (From lesson 7b)										
Use 'How much/many have you got?' Baseline assessment question 33 (From lesson 7e)										

Assessment for learning of Unit 8: There is a shower in the bathroom

Pupil name and understanding △ (see p. 14)

The pupil can successfully:	Names:									Notes for future planning
Use home vocabulary Baseline assessment question 34 (From lesson 8a)										
Use 'Are there/Is there . . . ? Yes, there is/No, there isn't (is not)' Baseline assessment question 35 (From lesson 8a)										
Use prepositions, e.g. in, on, under, next to, behind, between Baseline assessment question 36 (From lesson 8c)										

Assessment for learning of Unit 9: Can I have a glass of water please?   Names:

Pupil name and understanding △ (see p. 14)

The pupil can successfully:							Notes for future planning
Use feelings, e.g. thirsty, hungry, hot Baseline assessment question 37 (From lesson 9e)							
Make a request using 'I would like . . .?' Baseline assessment question 38 (From lesson 9d)							
Use 'Sorry, I don't understand, please, thank you, pardon' Not formally assessed (From lesson 9a)							
Use 'Do you have . . .? Yes, I do/No, I don't' Baseline assessment question 39 (From lesson 9b)							
Use 'Can I have . . .? Yes, you can/No, you can't' Baseline assessment question 40 (From lesson 9a)							
Use 'I want . . .' Baseline assessment question 41 (From lesson 9e)							

Assessment for learning of Unit 10: Where is the library?

Names:

Pupil name and understanding △ (see p. 14)

The pupil can successfully:								Notes for future planning
Use shops/places vocabulary								
Baseline assessment question 34								
(From lesson 10a)								
Use directions, e.g. turn left, turn right, straight on								
Baseline assessment question 42								
(From lesson 10c)								
Use 'Where is/are the . . . (Where's)'?								
Baseline assessment question 35								
(From lesson 10b)								
Use prepositions, e.g. in, on, under, next to, behind, in front of, near, between								
Baseline assessment question 36								
(From lesson 10b)								

Extended scale for EAL in England and Wales

Name:

	Listening	Speaking	Reading	Writing
Step 1	Pupil listens attentively for short bursts of time. They use non-verbal gestures to respond to greetings and questions about themselves, and they follow simple instructions based on the routines of the classroom.	Pupils echo words and expressions drawn from classroom routines and social interactions to communicate meaning. They express some basic needs using single words or phrases in English.	Pupils participate in reading activities. They know that, in English, print is read from left to right and from top to bottom. They recognise their names and familiar words and identify some letters of the alphabet by shape and sound.	Pupils use English letters and letter-like forms to convey meaning. They copy or write their names and familiar words, and write from left to right.
Step 2	Pupils understand simple conversational English. They listen and respond to the gist of general explanations by the teacher where language is supported by non-verbal cues, including illustrations.	Pupils copy talk that has been modelled. In their speech, they show some control of English word order and their pronunciation is generally intelligible.	Pupils begin to associate sounds with letters in English and to predict what the text will be about. They read words and phrases that they have learned in different curriculum areas. With support, they can follow a text read aloud.	Pupils attempt to express meanings in writing, supported by oral work or pictures. Generally their writing is intelligible to themselves and a familiar reader, and shows some knowledge of sound and letter patterns in English spelling. Building on their knowledge of literacy in another language, pupils show knowledge of the function of sentence division.
Level 1 (Threshold)	With support, pupils understand and respond appropriately to straightforward comments or instructions addressed to them.	Pupils speak about matters of immediate interest in familiar settings. They convey meaning through talk and gesture and can extend what they say with support.	Pupils can read a range of familiar words, and identify initial and final sounds in unfamiliar words. With support, they can establish meaning when reading aloud phrases or	Pupils produce recognisable letters and words in texts, which convey meaning and show some knowledge of English sentence division and word order. Most commonly used

Level	Speaking and listening	Reading	Writing
	Their speech is sometimes grammatically incomplete at word and phrase level.	simple sentences, and use contextual clues to gain understanding. They respond to events and ideas in poems, stories and non-fiction.	letters are correctly shaped, but may be inconsistent in their size and orientation.
Level 1 (Secure)	In familiar contexts, pupils follow what others say about what they are doing and thinking. They listen with understanding to sequences of instructions and usually respond appropriately in conversation. Pupils speak about matters of interest to a range of listeners and begin to develop connected utterances. What they say shows some grammatical complexity in expressing relationships between ideas and sequences of events. Pupils convey meaning, sustaining their contributions and the listeners' interest. They listen attentively to a range of speakers, including teacher presentation to the whole class.	Pupils use their knowledge of letters, sounds and words to establish meaning when reading familiar texts aloud, sometimes with prompting. They comment on events or ideas in poems, stories and non-fiction.	Pupils use phrases and longer statements which convey ideas to the reader, making some use of full stops and capital letters. Some grammatical patterns are irregular and pupils' grasp of English sounds and how they are written is not secure. Letters are usually clearly shaped and correctly orientated.
Level 2	Pupils begin to show confidence in talking and listening, particularly where the topics interest them. On occasions, they show awareness of the needs of the listener by including relevant detail. In developing and explaining their ideas they speak clearly and use a growing vocabulary. They usually listen carefully and respond with increasing appropriateness to what others say. They are beginning to be aware that in some situations a more formal vocabulary and tone of voice are used.	Pupils' reading of simple texts shows understanding and is generally accurate. They express opinions about major events or ideas in stories, poems and non-fiction. They use more than one strategy, such as phonic, graphic, syntactic and contextual, in reading unfamiliar words and establishing meaning.	Pupils' writing communicates meaning in both narrative and non-narrative forms, using appropriate and interesting vocabulary, and showing some awareness of the reader. Ideas are developed in a sequence of sentences, sometimes demarcated by capital letters and full stops. Simple, monosyllabic words are usually spelt correctly, and where there are inaccuracies the alternative is phonetically plausible. In handwriting, letters are accurately formed and consistent in size.

EAL optional planner

Unit: **Title:**   **Date:**

Day	Revision from previous lesson	Learning intention (grammar/vocabulary to be written on the board)	Speaking/listening activity	Independent/group activity (where possible, including mother tongue translation)	Plenary (including assessment for learning and writing new learning in Literacy Book)	Revision from a past lesson (this session can be done at any time)
Mon				Extension:		
Tues				Extension:		
Wed				Extension:		
Thurs				Extension:		
Fri				Extension:		

(these areas can be used for revision in future weeks)

Which learning intentions did the children find difficult?

Resources:

Example EAL optional planner

Unit: 5 **Title: Have you got any brothers or sisters?** **Date: 22 January**

Day	Revision from previous lesson	Learning intention (grammar/vocabulary to be written on the board)	Speaking/listening activity	Independent/group activity (where possible, including mother tongue translation)	Plenary (including assessment for learning and writing new learning in Literacy Book)	Revision from a past lesson (this session can be done at anytime)
Mon	Say different imperatives and get all the children to do this, e.g. stand up, jump	Family vocab., e.g. mum, dad, sister, brother 'How many brothers and sisters have you got?' 'I have got . . . brothers and . . . sisters.'	Write the learning intention on the board. Share family picture (5a). Write 'How many brothers and sisters have you got? I have got . . . brothers and . . . sisters.' In circle, ask the children, then ask the children to ask each other the question.	Make the family jigsaw (5b) and label family members. Extension: children make sentences using 'I have an older/younger brother/sister.'	Look at family picture (5a) and ask the children to guess what family member they can see.	Show animal pictures. Ask the children to name the animals. Ask them to use 'It's a' or 'It's an' when they speak. Play animal pairs.
Tues	Ask the children to ask each other how many brothers and sisters they have got.	Family vocab. and extended family, e.g. aunt, uncle, cousin, niece, nephew, husband, wife, son, daughter 'How many aunts and uncles have you got?' 'I have got . . . aunts and . . . uncles.'	Write the learning intention on the board. Ask children to think of all the members of the family and write them on the board. Give the children a family picture to look at without the labels (5a). Pupils pretend that they are 'Caroline Scott'. Work in pairs to decide relationships. Then the child pretends they are mum and looks at their relationships to her.	Pupils write: 'How many aunts do you have? I have got . . . aunts. How many cousins do you have? I have got . . .' cousins.' Extension: Use the sentence structure to ask other questions, e.g. 'How many pens/pencils have you got?'	Apply 'How many' to the classroom. Say, 'How many doors has it got?' Or 'How many pencils has . . . got?' Children can make up their own questions to apply their learning. Ask the children to bring in some photos of their family for the next lesson.	Use the cut up pronoun cards (3d). Ask the children to sit in a circle and take turns in turning over the pronoun cards. As each child turns a card, they must make a statement, e.g. 'He sleeps', 'I sleep'.

continued

Unit: 5 **Title: Have you got any brothers or sisters?** **Date: 22 January**

Day	Revision from previous lesson	Learning intention (grammar/vocabulary to be written on the board)	Speaking/listening activity	Independent/group activity (where possible, including mother tongue translation)	Plenary (including assessment for learning and writing new learning in Literacy Book)	Revision from a past lesson (this session can be done at anytime)
Wed	Show some photos of my family and say who the people are. Children use their family photos to identify their family members.	I have – I've She has – She's He has – He's It has – It's They have – They've We have – We've Caroline has – Caroline's You have – You've	Write the learning intention on the board. Read the long and short forms then read together. Write on the board: 'I've got 4 brothers.' 'I have got 4 brothers.' Ask the children how many brothers/aunts/uncles they have and expect an answer using the short form.	Write three sentences about their friends using the long form and the short form, e.g. He has got 4 brothers and no sisters. He's got 4 brothers and no sisters. She has got 3 aunts. She's got 3 aunts. Extension: Ask 'How many pets have they/he/she got?'	Each child uses their photo to say one sentence about a friend's family using the short form, e.g. He's got 3 sisters.	Show hobby pictures (6d) and pick some hobbies such as playing football (which would show liking PE), writing (which would show liking Literacy) and so on. Ask questions using the pictures, e.g. Does she like Literacy?
Thurs	Each child uses their photo to say one sentence about a friend's family using the short form, e.g. He's got 3 sisters.	This is my/her/his . . . . Who is this?	Write the learning intention on the board. Point to each pupil using their own photos and ask each child, 'Who is this?' Children introduce their families to each other saying, 'This is my . . .' Then write: 'This is my mother.' Then write: 'This is her/his . . .' Children swap photos and say 'This is her/his . . .'	Give photocopies of children's photos to each of the children. Each child sticks in someone else's family in their books and says who they are, e.g. This is his wife and son. Extension: Use 'their' family and our family have got 4 brothers or 3 aunts' to talk about different families.	Use resource sheet 5a and pupils pretend to be different members of the family so that they can then identify their relationship with each other.	Pick up two more items and ask who they belong to (his, hers, yours). Use resource sheet 1a to say, 'This is their cat', 'This is their baby'.

Fri		Description				
Use resource sheet 5a and pretend to be different members of the family so that they can then identify their relationship with each other.		Hair types Eye colour Hasn't got (has not got) Haven't got (have not got)	Write the learning intention on the board. Show descriptions (5d). Go round in a circle and children use two adjectives to describe their hair. Ask children to ask, 'Have you got blue hair? No, I haven't (have not)/ Yes, I have.'	Children complete resource sheet 5d and then write down: 'Has . . . got purple hair? No, she hasn't (has not). Has . . . got straight hair? Yes, he has.' Extension: More words to describe hair, e.g. frizzy, greasy, dry.	Children describe the characters on resource sheet 1a.	Children work in pairs and use groups of objects to explain the difference between, 'this, that, these, those'.

Which learning intentions did the children find difficult?
relationships between each of the family members, using the short forms

(these areas can be used for revision in future weeks)

Resources: New language ready to stick in their Remember Book, Family picture – resource sheet 5a, Family picture jigsaw – resource sheet 5b, Family questionnaire – resource sheet 5c, Descriptions – resource sheet 5d, Photos of my family, Animal word search – resource sheet 4b, Hobby pictures – resource sheet 6d , Subject labels – resource sheet 3a

Buddy sheet

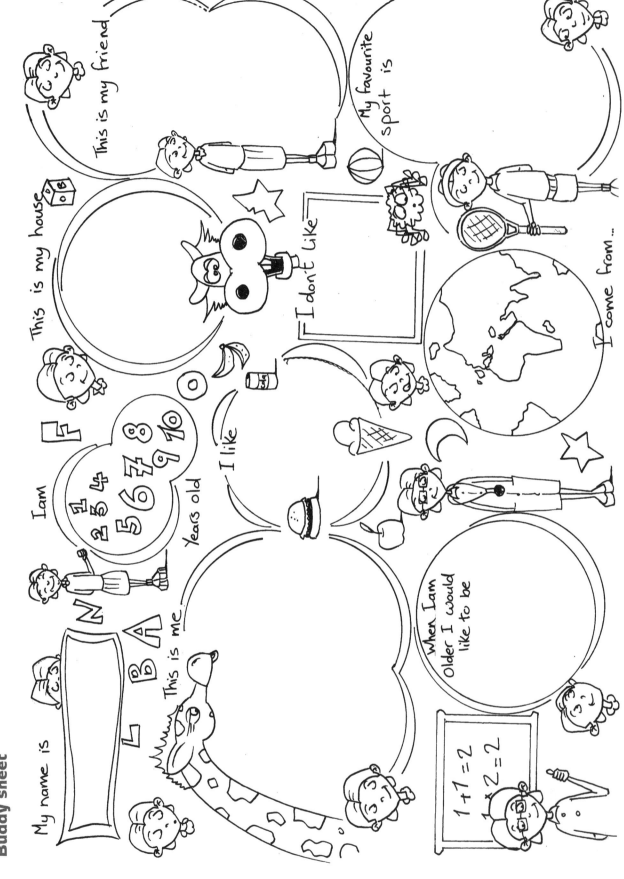

This is my friend

My favourite sport is

This is my house

I don't like

I come from...

I am
1 2 3 4
5 6 7 8
9 10
years old

I like

This is me

When I am older I would like to be

My name is

1 + 1 = 2
1 × 2 = 2

Useful words to remember

English	Your language
What's your name?	_____
My name is _____	_____
Yes	_____
No	_____
Please	_____
Thank you	_____
Sorry	_____
Hello	_____
Goodbye	_____
Have you finished?	_____
I have finished.	_____
I haven't finished.	_____
Do you understand?	_____
I understand.	_____
I don't understand.	_____
I don't know.	_____
Please can I go to the toilet?	_____
Can I go to the toilet?	_____
It's over there.	_____
I would like . . .	_____
Where is . . .?	_____
What is this?	_____
What is this/that in English?	_____

Why? _____

How? _____

When? _____

Which one? _____

Same _____

How many . . .? _____

+ (add, plus) _____

− (subtract, take away) _____

× (times, multiply) _____

= (equals) _____

Hot _____

Cold _____

Big _____

Small _____

Right _____

Wrong _____

Good _____

Bad _____

And _____

Go _____

Have _____

Be (is/am/are) _____

Can you . . .? _____

Is there . . .? _____

Have you got . . .? _____

See you soon. _____

Tidy up please. _____

Useful words to remember ☺

Yes/No

Thank you

Can I have a drink of water please?

Can I go to the toilet please?

Where is the . . .?

Do you have . . .?

I don't understand.

I don't know.

Can you say that again please?

Can you speak a little slower please?

What is this in English?

Why?

How?

When?

It is the same.

Is there . . .?

Have you got . . .?

How many . . .?

+ add   − take away   × times   ÷ divide

Characters – resource sheet 1a1

The Scott family

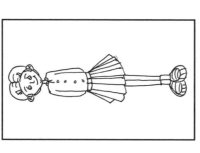

Caroline Scott

James Scott

Edd Scott

Helena Scott

Jon Scott

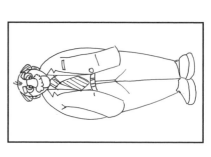

Iain Scott

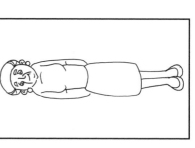

Sue Scott

Skippy

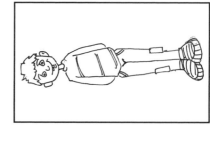

Friend Tom

Characters – resource sheet 1a2

The Matthew family

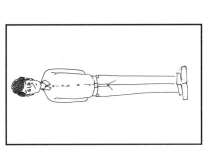

Steve Matthew

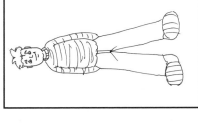

Nick Matthew

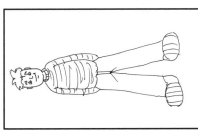

Trish Matthew

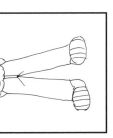

Lindsay Matthew

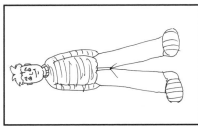

Adam Matthew

Rosie

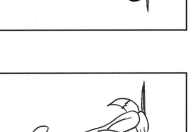

Jess

Characters – resource sheet 1a3

Some of the residents of Torrington Town

Name	Family	Age	Job	Personality	Look	Place of work
Iain Scott	Grandfather	59	Farmer	Grumpy, likes to sit in the armchair	Fat, glasses, oldish, grey hair, balding	Coombe View Farm
Sue Scott	Grandmother	55	Nurse	Caring, gentle	Maternal, oldish, short grey hair	Hospital
Helena Scott	Mum	36	Hairdresser	Gossip, always talking	Big beautiful hairdresser hair, slim	Helena's Hairdressers
Jon Scott	Dad	38	Policeman	Law abiding and sensible, quiet, never talks	Slim in suit/uniform	Police station
Caroline Scott	Me	10	At school	Mischievous, naughty, likes dancing, always happy	High bunched and A-line skirt, slim	Lawdale School
Edd Scott	Brother	7	At school	Likes computer games, lazy, watches TV a lot, moody and messy, looks sad	Big curly hair, a little bit fat	Lawdale School
Baby James	Baby brother	6 months		Cries a lot	Tuft of hair, fat	
Lindsay Matthew	Aunt	48	Doctor	Sensible, serious, likes reading	Straight, blonde, medium length hair, glasses and slim	Hospital
Adam Matthew	Uncle	49	Actor	Hippy, witty	Beard, a bit messy, a bit fat	Theatre
Steve Matthew	Cousin	25	Engineer	Likes swimming, eligible, dining out	Very tall and very thin, black hair	Office
Nick Matthew	Cousin	18	Unemployed	Likes football in Victoria Park with Steve, little bit fat, clumsy	Quite tall, blonde, well-built	
Trish Matthew	Cousin	12	At school	Likes listening to music, naughty (Caroline's best friend)	Long, black hair, trousers	Lawdale School
Tom George	Friend	8	At school	Likes to play the guitar, always happy (good friends with Edd)	Short, blonde hair, jeans and T-shirt	Lawdale School
Rosie	Pet dog			Sleepy	Lazy, huge dog!	
Jess	Pet dog			Lively, stupid	Black and white	

159

Colours poster – resource sheet 1c

Colour these things in the correct colours:

blue

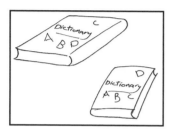

green

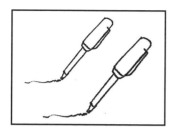

red

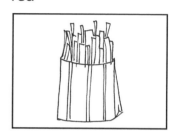

black

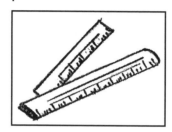

pink

orange

brown

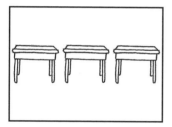

blue

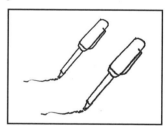

yellow

grey

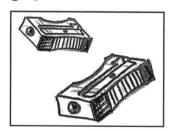

purple

white

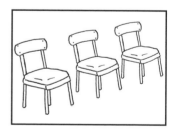

Visual labels for classroom – resource sheet 2a

pens

books

rulers

tables

rubbers

hole punch

board

pencils

dictionaries

scissors

paper

sharpeners

chairs

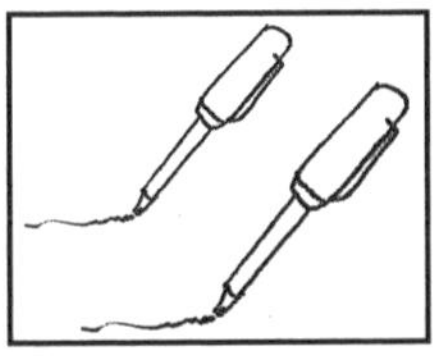

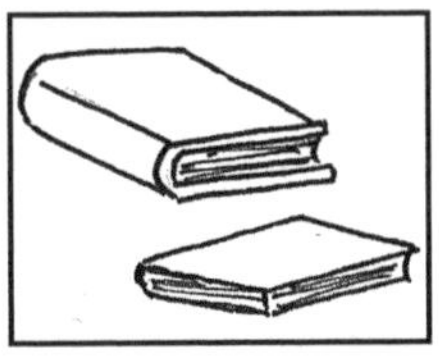

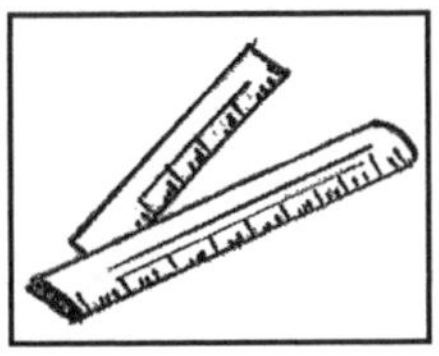

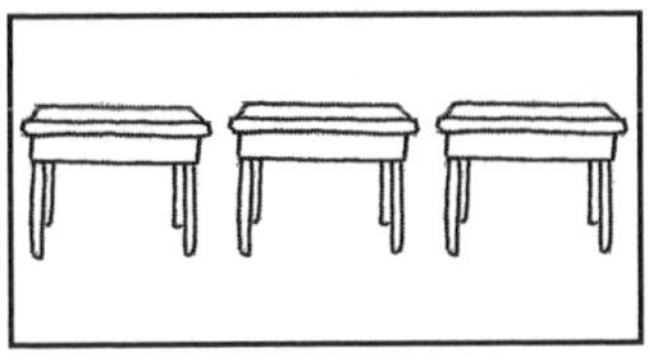

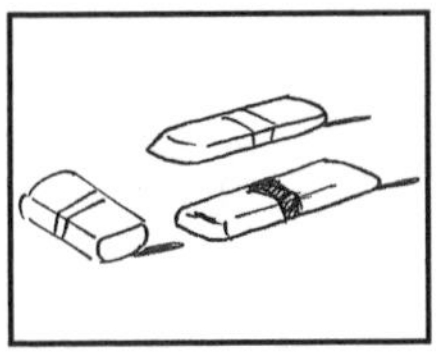

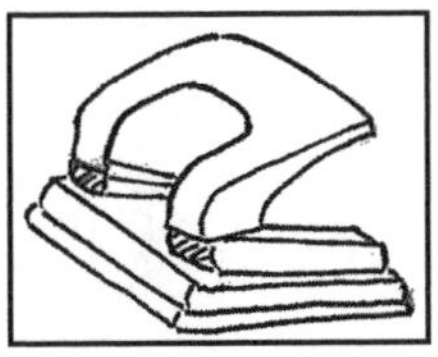

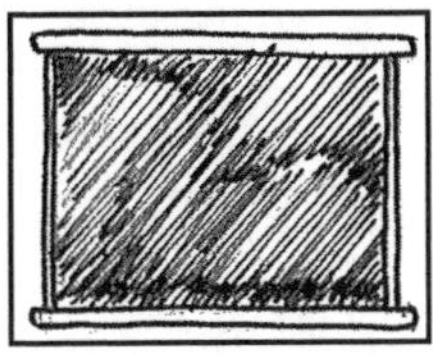

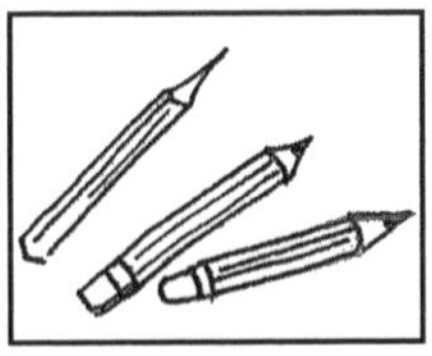

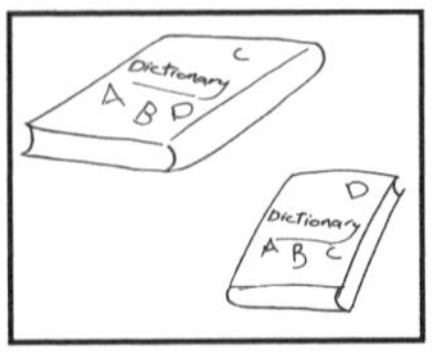

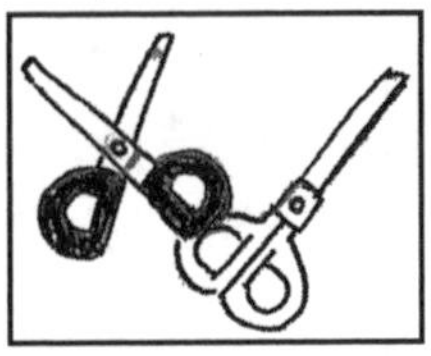

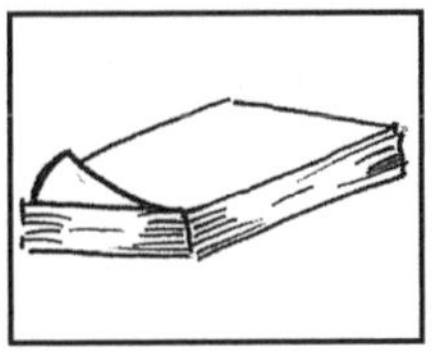

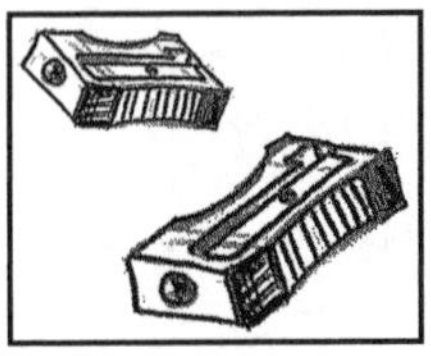

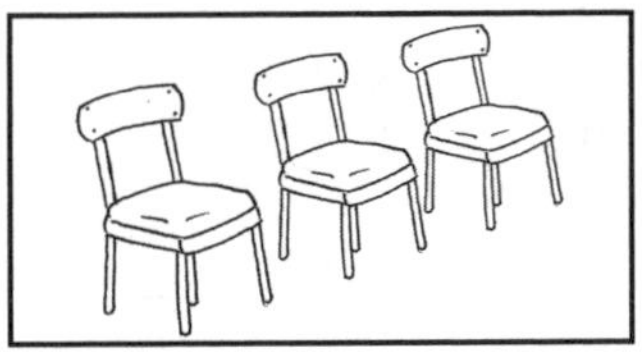

computers

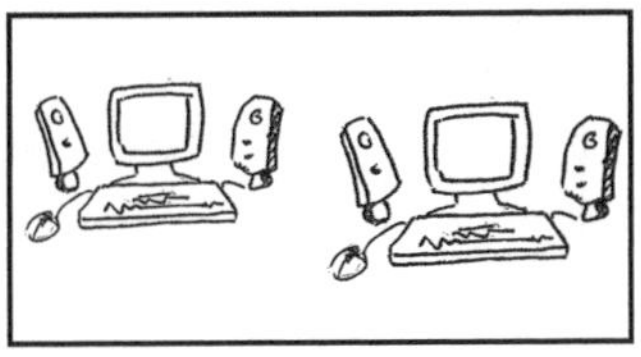

Numbers 1–100 – resource sheet 2b

one 1	two 2	three 3	four 4	five 5	six 6	seven 7	eight 8	nine 9	ten 10
eleven 11	twelve 12	thirteen 13	fourteen 14	fifteen 15	sixteen 16	seventeen 17	eighteen 18	nineteen 19	twenty 20
twenty-one 21	twenty-two 22	twenty-three 23	twenty-four 24	twenty-five 25	twenty-six 26	twenty-seven 27	twenty-eight 28	twenty-nine 29	thirty 30
thirty-one 31	thirty-two 32	thirty-three 33	thirty-four 34	thirty-five 35	thirty-six 36	thirty-seven 37	thirty-eight 38	thirty-nine 39	forty 40
forty-one 41	forty-two 42	forty-three 43	forty-four 44	forty-five 45	forty-six 46	forty-seven 47	forty-eight 48	forty-nine 49	fifty 50
fifty-one 51	fifty-two 52	fifty-three 53	fifty-four 54	fifty-five 55	fifty-six 56	fifty-seven 57	fifty-eight 58	fifty-nine 59	sixty 60
sixty-one 61	sixty-two 62	sixty-three 63	sixty-four 64	sixty-five 65	sixty-six 66	sixty-seven 67	sixty-eight 68	sixty-nine 69	seventy 70
seventy-one 71	seventy-two 72	seventy-three 73	seventy-four 74	seventy-five 75	seventy-six 76	seventy-seven 77	seventy-eight 78	seventy-nine 79	eighty 80
eighty-one 81	eighty-two 82	eighty-three 83	eighty-four 84	eighty-five 85	eighty-six 86	eighty-seven 87	eighty-eight 88	eighty-nine 89	ninety 90
ninety-one 91	ninety-two 92	ninety-three 93	ninety-four 94	ninety-five 95	ninety-six 96	ninety-seven 97	ninety-eight 98	ninety-nine 99	one hundred 100

Numeracy (Maths)

Literacy (English)

Geography

History

Physical Education (PE)

Art

Design and
Technology (D&T)

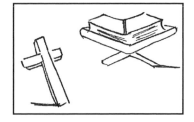

Religious Education (RE)

Information
Communication
Technology (ICT)

Music

Science

Do you like _____?

☺☺☺   I love_____

☺☺   I like _____

☹   _____ is OK.

☹☹   I don't like _____

☹☹☹   I hate _____

Subject

I _____

You _____

He _____

She _____

They _____

It _____

Verb

drink _____

walk _____

like _____

go _____

do _____

Object

to school _____

home _____

to the cinema _____

Example
Subject + Verb + Object
I + go + to school = I go to school.

I		You	
We		She	
He		It	
They		Caroline	

(sleep, walk, sit, eat, stand, watch TV, play football, say hello)

Animal matching – resource sheet 4a

Match these animals with their pictures:

lion

dog

cat

rabbit

mouse

horse

bird

fish

spider

elephant

cow

monkey

snake

giraffe

tiger

frog

crocodile

Animal word search – resource sheet 4b

Find these animals in the word search:

a	b	d	i	u	h	u	t	i	g	e	r
e	i	u	l	i	o	n	r	a	p	b	a
w	a	e	s	e	r	f	i	s	h	i	o
e	o	t	i	l	s	p	i	d	e	r	a
a	c	i	c	e	e	k	a	l	i	d	o
i	a	a	e	p	m	o	n	k	e	y	s
s	t	i	h	h	s	u	c	o	n	u	n
a	d	o	g	a	e	m	o	u	s	e	a
r	g	m	f	n	t	a	w	e	m	e	k
u	e	m	o	t	u	h	s	i	a	u	e
e	i	o	g	i	r	a	f	f	e	k	e
r	a	b	b	i	t	p	a	r	n	u	b

168

Animal word search – resource answer sheet 4b

a	b	d	i	u	h	u	t	i	g	e	r
e	i	u	l	i	o	n	r	a	p	b	a
w	a	e	s	e	r	f	i	s	h	i	o
e	o	t	i	l	s	p	i	d	e	r	a
a	c	i	c	e	e	k	a	l	i	d	o
i	a	a	e	p	m	o	n	k	e	y	s
s	t	i	h	h	s	u	c	o	n	u	n
a	d	o	g	a	e	m	o	u	s	e	a
r	g	m	f	n	t	a	w	e	m	e	k
u	e	m	o	t	u	h	s	i	a	u	e
e	i	o	g	i	r	a	f	f	e	k	e
r	a	b	b	i	t	p	a	r	n	u	b

At the zoo – resource sheet 4c

Fill in the gaps and draw your own in the last box.

Be careful of the _____

Don't feed the _____

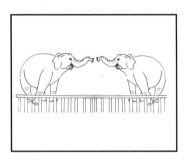

Don't walk with the _____

Watch the _____

Mind the _____

_____

Make your own:

_____

_____

170

Imperatives game – resource sheet 4d

Imperative cards:

Fill in the blanks with imperatives you would like to use.

Stand up	Sit down	Turn off the light	Put your hand up	Fold your arms
Point to the door	Add 5 and 2	Write your name	Shake the teacher's hand	

Use the game board below. Each child throws the dice and takes turns to move the number of places shown on the dice. If they land on an imperative, they must pick up an imperative card and complete the task. The winner is the first to finish.

Game

1. Start →	2. Imperative	3.	4.	5. Imperative	6.	7. Imperative	8.	9. Imperative
10. Imperative	11.	12. Imperative	13.	14.	15. Imperative	16.	17. Imperative	18.
19.	20. Imperative	21. Imperative	22.	23. Imperative	24.	25. Imperative	26. →	Finish

Family questionnaire – resource sheet 5c

How many _____ have you got?

Name	brothers	sisters	cousins	uncles	aunts
Caroline	4	0	8	4	4

1. _____ has got _____ brothers.

2. _____ has got _____ sisters.

3. _____ has got _____ uncles.

4. _____

5. _____

174

Draw the descriptions below:

| blonde | brown hair | black hair | grey hair | long hair |

| short hair | curly hair | straight hair | wavy hair | bald |

| blue eyes | brown eyes | black eyes | moustache | beard |

Sports Questionnaire

Write questions using 'Do you like_____ (a sport)?' Then ask your friends.

Questions:	How many people like it?
Example: Do you like football?	

Sports word search – resource sheet 6b

Find the sports pictured below in the word search:

s	b	a	d	m	i	n	t	o	n	b	v	r	t	w
w	b	d	b	c	d	s	b	f	g	a	o	t	s	a
i	o	f	o	o	t	b	a	l	l	s	l	n	p	l
m	b	o	e	d	h	t	s	t	n	k	l	l	u	k
m	a	w	g	g	k	s	e	o	n	e	e	w	m	i
i	c	h	p	v	d	d	b	l	m	t	y	t	a	n
n	y	u	f	h	w	c	a	p	p	b	b	e	s	g
g	r	e	i	o	m	h	l	s	r	a	a	c	k	s
s	k	a	t	i	n	g	l	o	n	l	l	y	i	p
c	f	s	g	d	a	e	t	k	s	l	l	c	i	a
t	a	b	l	e	t	e	n	n	i	s	m	l	n	t
c	a	t	e	n	n	i	s	s	c	d	f	i	g	n
i	e	o	h	b	o	d	j	c	d	m	g	n	b	a
g	y	m	n	a	s	t	i	c	s	l	b	g	c	n
r	u	n	n	i	n	g	c	s	q	u	a	s	h	e

   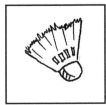 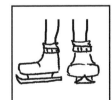

Sports word search – resource answer sheet 6b

s	b	a	d	m	i	n	t	o	n	b	v	r	t	w
w	b	d	b	c	d	s	b	f	g	a	o	t	s	a
i	o	f	o	o	t	b	a	l	l	s	l	n	p	l
m	b	o	e	d	h	t	s	t	n	k	l	l	u	k
m	a	w	g	g	k	s	e	o	n	e	e	w	m	i
i	c	h	p	v	d	d	b	l	m	t	y	t	a	n
n	y	u	f	h	w	c	a	p	p	b	b	e	s	g
g	r	e	i	o	m	h	l	s	r	a	a	c	k	s
s	k	a	t	i	n	g	l	o	n	l	l	y	i	p
c	f	s	g	d	a	e	t	k	s	l	l	c	i	a
t	a	b	l	e	t	e	n	n	i	s	m	l	n	t
c	a	t	e	n	n	i	s	s	c	d	f	i	g	n
i	e	o	h	b	o	d	j	c	d	m	g	n	b	a
g	y	m	n	a	s	t	i	c	s	l	b	g	c	n
r	u	n	n	i	n	g	c	s	q	u	a	s	h	e

178

Label first and second:

Label first, second and third:

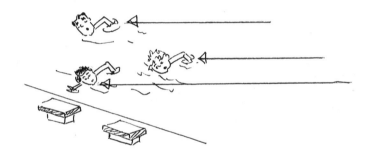

Label the order they finished:

Hobby pictures – resource sheet 6d

  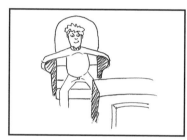

playing guitar	dancing	writing	cooking
playing on the computer	going to the cinema	listening to music	playing games
watching television	talking on the telephone	playing sport	playing football
drawing	reading	singing	

A–Z food – resource sheet 7a

a _____

b _____

c _____

d _____

e _____

f _____

g _____

h _____

i _____

j _____

k _____

l _____

m _____

n _____

o _____

p _____

q _____

r _____

s _____

t _____

u _____

v _____

w _____

x _____

y _____

z _____

Food pictures – resource sheet 7b

chips   potatoes   rice   pasta   bread   cheese

yoghurt   hamburger   pizza   crisps   chocolate   fizzy drinks

biscuits   chicken   cake

ham	cucumber	grapes	fish	courgette
prawn	egg	milk	tea	coffee
lemon	water	banana	tomato	onion

Classifiers – resource sheet 7c

a bottle of	a packet of	a can of
a piece of	a glass of	a bowl of
a loaf of	a carton of	a bag of

a tin of	a slice of
a plate of	a jar of
a cup of	a jug of

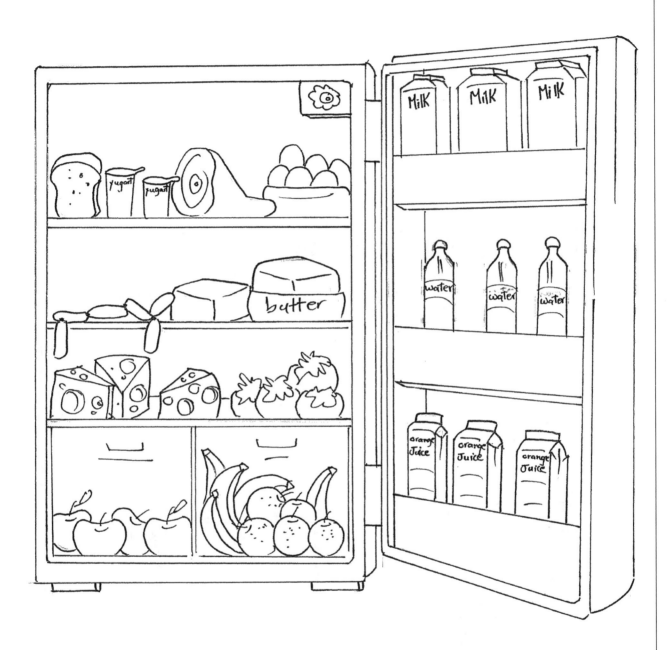

185

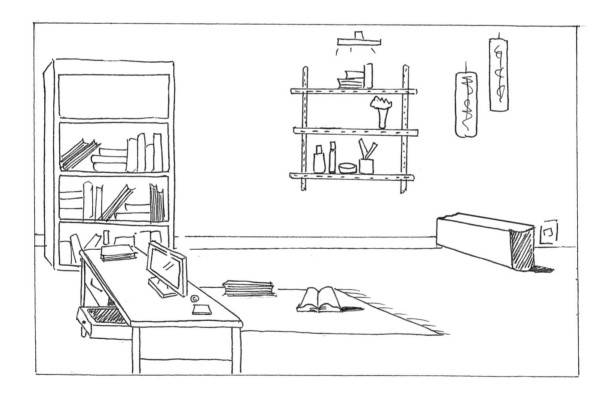

Spider prepositions – resource sheet 8c

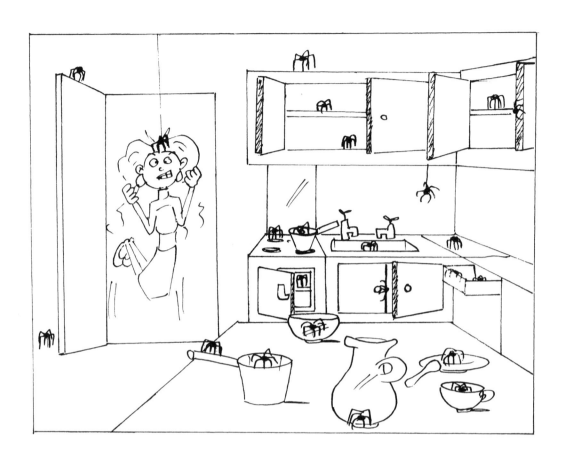

Home Vocabulary

jug
sink
cupboard
door
drawer
bowl
pan
spoon
saucer
cup
table
oven
stove
shelf

Preposition Vocabulary

on
in
above
over
under
next to
beside
near
in front of
behind

Can I go to the toilet please?	
Can I borrow your pen please?	
Can you pass me the plate please?	
Can you help me please?	
Can I have something to eat please?	
Can I have something to drink please?	
Can you take me to my classroom please?	

I'm tired.		I'm thirsty.	
I'm hungry.		I'm hot.	
I'm late.		I'm cold.	
I'm bored.		I'm wet.	

I want a drink.		I want some food.	
I want to put my jumper on.		I want to go swimming.	
I want to be quick.		I want to play.	
I want to get dry.		I want to go to bed.	

191

Pictures of shops – resource sheet 10a

cinema	restaurant	newsagents	station	bank
library	supermarket	pharmacy	school	park
shoe shop	jewellers	market	theatre	hairdressers

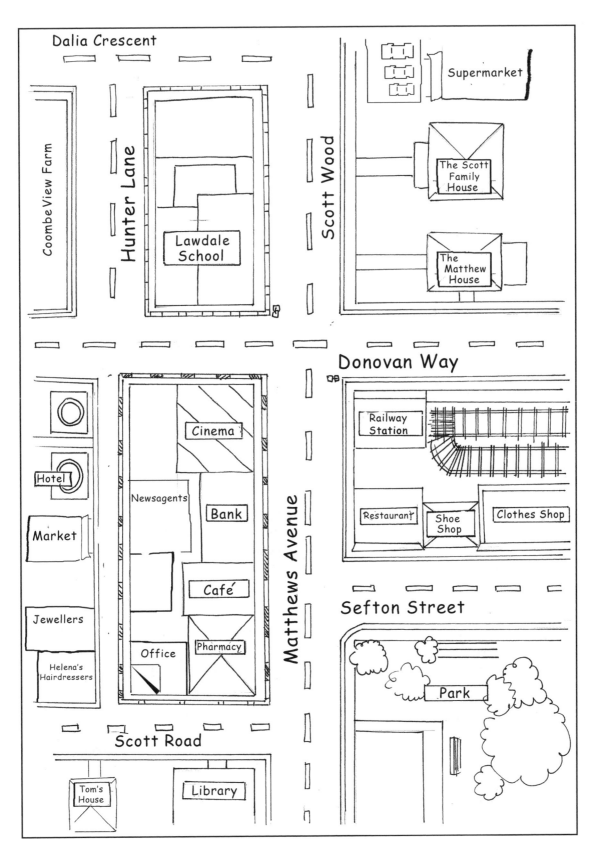

193

Adjective
A word that describes somebody or something. It describes a noun. It normally comes before a noun, e.g. <u>big</u> horse or <u>blue</u> car.

Adverb
A word that describes a verb.

Article
This is a type of determiner (a class of words occurring before a noun). There is a definite article which is 'the' or the indefinite article which is 'a' and 'an'.

Apostrophe
The symbol ('). 1. Used to indicate missing letters, e.g. I've. 2. Used to indicate possession, e.g. The girl's socks – the apostrophe is placed before the s. When the noun is plural already, the apostrophe is placed after the s, e.g. The girls' socks.

Baseline assessment
To assess what a child already knows and can do on entering a school. A non-graded test is used for this.

Cardinal number
A number, e.g. one, two, three.

Clause
A section of a sentence that contains a subject and a verb.

Countable noun
A noun that has both a plural and a singular form, e.g. a pig, two pigs.

Determiner
A group of words that fall before the noun, e.g. a, an, some, this, the.

Formative assessment
This indicates stages reached, which then helps to identify areas of subsequent work and development.

High frequency words
The most used words. These words are therefore very useful to the learner.

Infinitive
The basic form of a verb, e.g. to see, to sleep.

Kinaesthetic
A word used to describe activities that involve bodily movement. Kinaesthetic learners need to learn by doing.

New arrival
In this case, a pupil new to a school who speaks little or no English.

Noun
A word used to refer to somebody or something. A noun includes names of people, animals, objects, substances, events and feelings. Nouns can be divided into two groups: countable and uncountable.

Object
A noun or pronoun that normally comes after the verb in a clause containing an action verb, e.g. break, told. In 'Trish sees the dog', 'Trish' is the subject and 'the dog' is the object.

Ordinal number
A number defining a noun's position, e.g. first, second, third.

Plural
More than one.

Possessive adjective
These are determiners such as my, her, his, its, their, our, your.

Pronoun
A noun used instead of the name of someone who is already mentioned, e.g. he, she, this.

Punctuation
Marks that help readers interpret text.

Sentence
A complete set of words that have meaning. Sentences normally have one or more clauses and usually at least one subject and verb. A simple sentence is a sentence with one clause only, e.g. I was early.

Singular
Only one of something.

Subject
The subject is the 'what' or 'who' that the sentence is about.

Syllable
The beat of a word, e.g. el – e – phant.

Tense
A word used to describe time of action, happening or process highlighted by the verb, e.g. past – went, present – go and future – will go.

Third person
Used to talk about a third party, e.g. he, she.

Uncountable noun
For example, water, milk, wood or air. These nouns usually have no plural forms.

Verb
A word used to describe an action, state or occurrence. Often described as a 'doing' or 'being' word, e.g. shout, become.

Vocabulary
Words used for specific language, e.g. transport vocabulary.

Vowel
The five vowels are a, e, i, o, u. Every syllable contains a vowel sound.

Abbreviations

EAL – English as an Additional Language
ICT – Information Communication Technology
TA – Teaching Assistant
QCA – Qualifications and Curriculum Authority

Bibliography

Barnett, A., Stainthorp, R., Henderson, S. and Scheib, B. (2006) *Handwriting Policy and Practice in English Primary Schools,* London: University of London Institute of Education

Beaumont, D. (1993) *Elementary English Grammar: An Elementary Reference and Practice Book*, Basingstoke: Macmillan Heinemann

Black, P. and Wiliam, D. (1998) 'Assessment and classroom learning', *Assessment in Education*, 5(1): 7–74

Black, P. and Wiliam, D. (1998) *Inside the Black Box: Raising Standards Through Classroom Assessment*, London: King's College School of Education

Brain Gym, www.braingym.org

Clarke, S. (2001) *Unlocking Formative Assessment: Practical Strategies for Enhancing Pupils' Learning in the Primary Classroom*, London: Hodder & Stoughton

Danise, B. (2001) *Scaffolding: Teaching and Learning in Language and Literacy Education*, Newtown, New South Wales: Primary English Teaching Association

DETE (Department for Education, Training and Employment) (nd) 'ESL in the mainstream for the early learner: partcipants' manual', online: www.decs.sa.gov.au/curric/files/links/08_ESLM_for_the_Early_Lear.pdf

DfES (Department for Education and Science) (2002) 'Supporting pupils learning English as an additional language', online: www.standards.dfes.gov.uk/primary/publications/literacy/63381/

DfES (2004) *Learning and Teaching in the Primary Years* (ref DfES0518-2004G), London: DfES

DfES (2005) *Guidance on Implementation of the KS2 Framework for Languages* (ref DfES1721-2005-EN), London: DfES

DfES (2006a) *Excellence and Enjoyment: Learning and Teaching for Bilingual Children in the Primary Years. Unit 1: Planning and Assessment for Language and Learning* (Primary National Strategy, ref 2132-2006DCL-EN), London: DfES

DfES (2006b) *Primary Framework for Literacy and Mathematics Learning* (Primary National Strategy, ref 02011-2006BOK-EN), London: DfES

Edwards, A. and Warin, J. (1999) 'Parental involvement in raising the achievement of primary school pupils: why bother?', *Oxford Review of Education*, 25(3): 325–341

Gardner, H. (1999) *Intelligence Reframed: Multiple Intelliences for the 21st Century*, New York: Basic Books

Gibbons, P. (1991) *Learning to Learn in a Second Language*, Newtown, New South Wales: Primary English Teaching Association

Gillies, R.M. (2004) 'The effects of cooperative learning on junior high school students during small group learning', *Learning and Instruction*, 14(2): 197–213

Hall, D. (2001) *Assessing the Needs of Bilingual Children: Living in Two Languages*, London: David Fulton

Hallam, S., Ireson, J. and Davies, J. (2004) 'Primary pupils' experiences of different types of grouping in school', *British Educational Research Journal*, 30(4): 516–533

Institute of Education (2006) 'Handwriting lessons important but ignored, finds survey', online: http://ioewebserver.ioe.ac.uk/ioe/cms/get.asp?cid=1397&1397_1=14041

Marion. T. (2005) 'How do the teacher's gestures help the young children in second language acquisition?' paper presented at 2nd ISGS Conference, Lyon, France, 15–18 June, online: http://gesture-lyon2005.ens-lsh.fr/IMG/pdf/Livret_resumes.pdf

Murphy, R. (1998) *Essential Grammar in Use*, Cambridge: Cambridge University Press

QCA (2000) *A Language in Common: Assessing English as an Additional Language* (ref QCA/00/584), London: QCA

QCA (2004a) *Introductory Guides: Learning and Teaching in the Primary Years* (ref DfES0243-2004G), London: QCA

QCA (2004b) 'Pathways to learning for new arrivals', online: www.qca.org.uk/qca_7526.aspx

QCA (2005) *Approaches to Language Teaching in Key Stage 2* (ref DfES1721-2005-EN), London: QCA

QCA (2006) *Excellence and Enjoyment: Learning and Teaching for Bilingual Children in Primary Years. Professional Development Materials* (ref 0013-2006PCK-EN), London: QCA

QCA (2007) *Teaching Units to Support Guided Sessions for Writing in EAL* (pilot material, ref 00068-2007FLR-EN), London: QCA

Rees, D., Honeychurch, C., Clayton, J., Polias, J. and Dare, B. (2002) *ESL in the Mainstream for Early Learner*, Canberra: DETE Publishing

Smith, A. and Call, N. (2001)*The Alps Approach Resource Book*, Stafford: Network Educational Press

Swan, M. (1995) *Practical English Usage*, Oxford: Oxford University Press

Swan, M. and Walter, C. (1997) *How English Works: A Grammar Practice Book*, Oxford: Oxford University Press

Tellier, M. (2005) 'How do teacher's gestures help young children in second language acquisition?', online: http://gesture-lyon2005.ens-lsh.fr/article.php3?id_article=253

Torrance, H. and Pryor, J. (2001) 'Developing formative assessment in the classroom; using action research to explore and modify theory. How can classroom assessment be used to support children's learning?', *British Educational Research Journal*, 27(5): 615–631.

Ward, G. (2003) *Key Strategies for a Language Enhancing Curriculum: Beginners to English*, online: homepage.ntlworld.com/gordon.ward2000/E-A-L/beginners/BEGINNER-advice.DOC

Wilson, V., Schlapp, U. and Davidson, J. (2003) 'An "extra pair of hands"? Managing classroom assistants in Scottish primary schools', *Educational Management and Administration*, 31(2): 189–205

Index